THE JEWELRY AND ENAMELS OF
Louis Comfort Tiffany

Janet Zapata

THE JEWELRY AND ENAMELS OF
Louis Comfort Tiffany

HARRY N. ABRAMS, INC., PUBLISHERS

**For my mother, Doris Armstrong, whose gentle spirit
has always guided me**

Library of Congress Cataloging-in-Publication Data

Zapata, Janet.
    The jewelry and enamels of Louis Comfort Tiffany / by Janet
Zapata.
       p.   cm.
    ISBN 0–8109–3506–6
    1. Tiffany, Louis Comfort, 1848–1933—Criticism and
interpretation.   2. Jewelry—United States—History—20th century—
Themes, motives.   3. Enamel and enameling—United States—
History—20th century—Themes, motives.   4. Tiffany and Company.
I. Tiffany, Louis Comfort, 1848–1933. II. Title.
NK7398.T5Z36 1993
739.27′092—dc20   93–7309
                                                          CIP

Published in 1993 by
Harry N. Abrams, Incorporated, New York
A Times Mirror Company

Printed and bound in Singapore

Contents

1

Louis Comfort Tiffany:
The Man and the Artist

Although there has been much recent scholarship regarding the work of Louis Comfort Tiffany, the role he played at Tiffany & Co. has remained an enigma. His work in glass, ceramics, bronze, stained glass windows and leaded glass lamps has been well documented. A few authors have tried to decipher his involvement in enameling and jewelry; however, very important questions remain open, and considerable confusion has resulted from the lack of a rigorous chronology of his work in this area. For example, *The Art of Louis Comfort Tiffany*, ghostwritten in 1914 by the *New York Times* art and literary critic, Charles DeKay, includes a chapter on these aspects of Tiffany's output but only skims the surface and makes no attempt to sort out the differences between the pieces executed at Tiffany Furnaces and those made at Tiffany & Co.

With the help of newly discovered material, the present book analyzes the development of Louis Tiffany's jewelry and enameled objects from their early conception, when they were produced at Tiffany Furnaces, through the consolidation at Tiffany & Co. until the department's closing in 1933. To better understand and appreciate the import of Tiffany's œuvre, this first chapter traces his early life, where the roots of his inspiration and aesthetic principles were established and developed.

Louis Comfort Tiffany was the son of Charles L. Tiffany, a co-founder of Tiffany & Co. His preference for an artistic career rather than the mercantile opportunities offered by his father's business could have been a disappointment to the elder Tiffany. In reality, just the opposite was true. When considering the backgrounds of both men, we find similarities in their personalities. Charles, like his son, had taken a path separate from his own father's and would, therefore, have been sympathetic to his son's desire to pursue his own dream. Both men were driven to achieve the seemingly impossible in their own chosen field of activity, setting higher standards for their work than one would consider attainable. They both specialized in creating and selling beauty; they differed only in their conception of what the art object should look like. One was more interested in making money out of art, the other in creating art that would last and be appreciated for generations.

Charles supported his son's creative enterprises in a number of direct ways. He invested in several, if not all, of Louis's companies;[1] and he also relinquished space in his own company's exhibits at several international exhibitions so that Louis could display his latest artistic achievements. That they loved and respected each other there can be no doubt.

My opinion concurs with that of Gertrude Speenburgh who wrote in *The Arts of the Tiffanys*, ''There seems to have been a bond of sympathy between the father and the son, for the young artist was enabled by the remarkable success of his father's commercial enterprises to travel and study abroad, and eventually to launch himself in his chosen field.''[2] Many years after Louis achieved international fame, George Frederick Kunz, the Tiffany & Co. gemologist who worked intimately with both Charles and Louis Tiffany, reflected on the special relationship between father and son: ''His father's profession had no attraction for him, and the father, with much foresight, allowed the young man to gratify his artistic taste.''[3]

Charles Lewis Tiffany was the son of Chloe and Comfort Tiffany of Danielson, Connecticut. His father was a co-founder and partner in the Danielson Manufacturing Company, one of the first cotton mills in that state. After twenty years in the business, he sold his rights and opened a competitive mill across the river, known as the Brooklyn Manufacturing Company. At the same time he opened a country store to service the needs of his employees. This proved to be a shrewd maneuver on his part, for he not only reaped benefits from his employees' labor but also profited from their purchases. He interrupted his son's studies at nearby Plainfield Academy, a private secondary school, to give him full responsibility for running the store, doing everything from purchasing merchandise, selling to customers, journeying to New York City to replenish his stock, and balancing account ledgers. In spite of very little mercantile background, Charles succeeded within a year in increasing revenues to such an extent that he could hire an assistant and return to his education.

After graduating from school, he spent seven years in the store learning the basics of retailing. It was here that he laid the foundation for his future success. Working in a small town and catering to the same customers daily imbued him with such commonsense attributes as courtesy, integrity, and punctuality.[4] This background was to stand him in good stead for the remainder of his life.

1. A humidor designed by Louis Comfort Tiffany around 1901. The spiral motif serves not only as an embellishment but also as a framework for the favrile glass of the body.

2, 3. The dragonfly was a motif
Tiffany used on lamps and jewelry;
he may have been introduced to it
by his mentor, Edward C. Moore.
For instance, the dragonfly was
used by Moore for Tiffany & Co.
around 1878 on the silver vase
with applied decoration in gold
and copper at left. *(Collection of
the Brooklyn Museum, H.
Randolph Lever Fund)*. The motif
on Louis Comfort Tiffany's
chandelier, above, is similar in its
application.

4. This scent bottle, to which Tiffany contributed the favrile glass vessel while Paulding Farnham designed the elaborate gold stopper set with Mexican fire opals, diamonds and rubies, was shown in the Tiffany & Co. display at the 1900 Exposition Universelle in Paris. *(Private collection).*

5. The bronze wirework on the feet of this lamp designed around 1900 encases favrile glass balls, a technique which was to appear again later in Tiffany's jade jewelry.

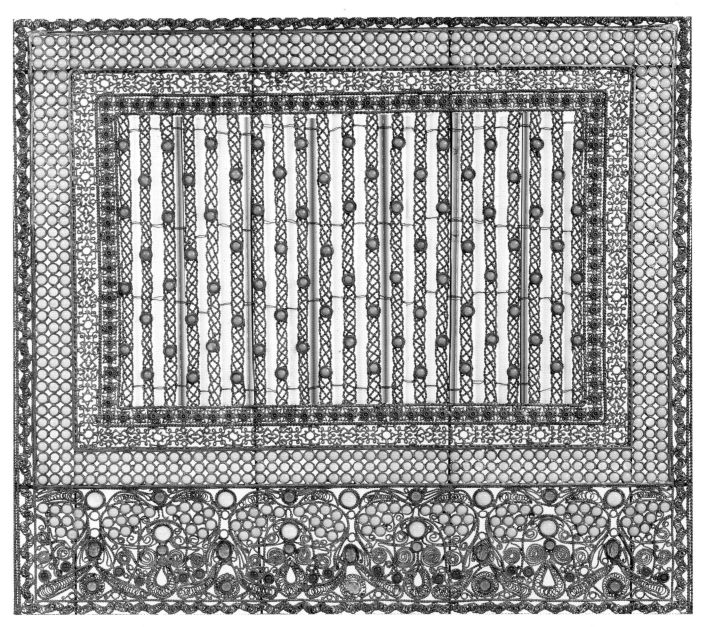

6. The gilt bronze fireplace screen in the Havemeyer house was made of opalescent glass rods and balls, and shows an interesting play of solid shapes with intricate filigree work. *(University of Michigan School of Art and College of Architecture and Urban Planning, on extended loan to the University of Michigan Museum of Art).*

7. Included in Louis Comfort Tiffany's chapel at the 1893 World's Columbian Exposition in Chicago was this benediction candelabrum decorated with opalescent glass. *(Photograph courtesy Nicholas M. Dawes).*

Comfort Tiffany eventually bought out his partners in the cotton mill with the intention of going into business with his son and renaming the company C. Tiffany & Son. But Charles had other ideas. With all the passionate optimism of a brash and courageous pioneer, Charles Tiffany decided at the age of 25 to leave behind his Connecticut roots and conquer new horizons in bustling New York City. His boyhood friend, John B. Young, had already ventured into the city, where he worked in a stationery and dry goods store for six months. Banking on their background experience and determination to succeed, the friends decided to form a partnership in a store similar to the one in which Young had been employed. They opened their first store, known as Tiffany & Young, at 259 Broadway on 21 September 1837 during a period of economic panic when hundreds of businesses were closing their doors. In spite of the general tenor of the times, Tiffany and Young surged ahead, prospering in the midst of the recession. Their first day's sales amounted to only $4.98; by the third day their receipts had risen to $24.31. During their first week of business, the partners remained in the black, with a meager profit of only 33 cents; however, they were surviving where others had failed. The stock they first offered included papier-mâché articles, terracotta ware, umbrellas, desks, walking sticks, dressing cases and stationery.[5]

Charles Tiffany soon realized that he could increase profits by offering quality items. He scouted the ships arriving from abroad, purchasing articles that came from exotic places like Japan and China. These were quickly sold and his only regret was that he had not bought more. At the same time, Tiffany & Young established a one-price system, in contrast to other retailers who haggled over prices. Although this policy does not seem revolutionary today, at the time it was a daring venture that paid off in profits and consumer confidence.

On 30 November 1841, Tiffany married his partner's sister, Harriet Olivia Young. That same year the partners accepted Jabez L. Ellis into the company, and the name was changed to Tiffany, Young & Ellis. This move brought in additional capital that enabled John Young to travel to Europe in order to procure the latest merchandise, such as paste jewelry from Hanau, Germany, and "Palais Royale" from Paris. The latter incorporated paste diamonds in elegant settings, and was an instant success. This encouraged the company to offer gold jewelry from Paris, London, Florence and Rome in 1845. With the continuing expansion of their business, the premises at 259 Broadway were found to be too small, and so in 1847 they moved to 271 Broadway.

The year 1848 was a turning point for the fledgling company. During John Young's annual trip to France, instead of buying the usual fancy goods and gold jewelry for the store, he took advantage of the tempestuous political atmosphere and purchased diamonds at half their value from deposed

8. The rope twist motif on this early chandelier made at Tiffany Studios became a dominant decorative element in Tiffany's jewelry.

dignitaries in search of ready cash. With this cache of gemstones, the partners embarked upon a new venture, the manufacture of gold jewelry. Heretofore, Tiffany, Young & Ellis had merely been retailers, never stepping into the area of manufacturing. The acquisition of diamonds and other precious stones from Parisian nobility (Tiffany reputedly also bought Marie Antoinette's girdle of diamonds) gave the company a ready supply of stones for their jewelry, as well as a regal provenance to heighten their mystique. Up to this time, Ball, Thompkins & Black were considered *the* prestigious New York firm offering fine gemstone jewelry. Charles Tiffany was aware of the economic growth in the country that resulted from the Industrial Revolution. As a keen businessman, he realized the potential for becoming one of the few jewelers in the city able to provide fine jewels for this newly rich class, who looked for ways to flaunt their wealth.

Towards the beginning of this pivotal year for Tiffany, Young & Ellis, Harriet and Charles's second son, Louis Comfort, was born on 18 February.[6] It is interesting to note that Louis Tiffany entered the world in the same year that his father's firm embarked on the serious business of manufacturing jewelry.

An admirer of Louis Tiffany's jewelry oeuvre cannot help speculating as to why it took him so long to get started in a field to which he had so much to contribute. The question is even more intriguing when one considers that his father's business provided what would appear to be an ideally nurturing environment for developing a talent in this field. To begin to answer this question, one has to follow in some detail the evolution of Tiffany & Co. as young Louis Tiffany was growing up.

The late 1840s was also a period when Tiffany, Young & Ellis embarked into another area which, like jewelry, quickly became the mainstay of their business. At about the same time that they started manufacturing fine jewelry, they decided to expand their stock to include European silverware. The exact year in which this took place is not known. Charles and Mary Grace Carpenter speculate in *Tiffany Silver* that it was either 1847 or 1848. The new line proved to be successful until a high protective tariff forced the company to turn to American-made silver. In 1851 they contracted with John C. Moore to produce silver exclusively for Tiffany's. Moore retired shortly thereafter and his son, Edward Chandler Moore, took over management of his father's company, thus starting his association with Tiffany's.

The change in direction from a small stationery and fancy goods store to a prominent jewelry and silver house was probably more than John Young and Jabez Ellis had bargained for when they embarked on the initial business endeavor. In 1853, Charles Tiffany bought out his partners and changed the company name to Tiffany & Co. By this date, the company had moved twice and was now located further uptown, at 550 Broadway.

As Charles Tiffany assumed control of the company, he organized it in a vertical structure, with himself at the helm and selected competent individuals taking charge of specific areas. In 1850, he formed a partnership with Gideon F. T. Reed, formerly of the Boston jewelers Lincoln, Reed & Co., to open an office in Paris, located at 79 rue de Richelieu, that became known as Tiffany & Reed. From this location, Reed was able to purchase diamonds and other precious stones for the New York store. By 1851, Tiffany had designated the John C. Moore Company, with Edward Moore in charge, as the principal manufacturer of Tiffany silver, although the firm continued to retail silverware by other makers.

Under this new arrangement, Edward Moore became the dominant designer for Tiffany & Co.'s silverware. His shop was not located within the premises of Tiffany & Co., but at 55 Prince Street. At the outset of this working relationship, the silverware Moore produced was designed in the conventional revival styles of the period, such as chinoiserie, rococo, Renaissance, and neo-classical. For the most part, Moore continued making silver in these styles until 1 May 1868, when a business transaction occurred that changed the course of Tiffany silver forever. On that date, Tiffany & Co. incorporated and absorbed the John C. Moore Company within the firm. Edward Moore received shares in Tiffany & Co. and became a trustee on its Board of Directors.

There are no surviving records to determine whether this agreement signified increased financial benefits for the silver plant; in a short period, however, many new and exciting designs emerged from the shop. Within a year after the amalgamation, Moore patented his first flatware pattern, *Tiffany*. It was followed by *Italian*, *Antique*, *Cook* and *Queen Anne* in 1870, *Palm* and *Japanese* in 1871, and *Vine* and *Persian* in 1872.[7] In the space of four years, Moore introduced nine new flatware patterns, a feat almost unimaginable in such a short period.

Holloware followed suit. No longer would Tiffany silver follow the dictates of current styles. Under Moore's capable direction, Tiffany & Co. became the leader in American silver with the introduction of Japonism into its repertoire. Silver no longer had to be strictly utilitarian: it was now designed as a work of art and was recognized as such at the 1878 Exposition Universelle in Paris, where Tiffany's received top honors, to the shock of European critics.

Edward Moore was a private person; little is known about his life or his working relationship with Tiffany & Co. In keeping with the traditional Tiffany policy of designer anonymity, his creations were all credited to Tiffany & Co., with the exception of his flatware patterns and the drawings of presentation swords executed after the Civil War. He acted as head of his division, with full control over every object designed under his supervision. From an idea, he would instruct his designers to make a drawing which he would then approve, signing it with his initials. Many drawings in the Tiffany archives bear his approval signature. Louis Comfort Tiffany was to follow the same procedure after he established his own jewelry and enameling division at Tiffany & Co.

When analyzing the professional lives of Edward Moore and Louis Tiffany, we find correspondences in their artistic practises, collecting habits and design credo. Many sources have credited Moore as a likely mentor for the young Tiffany, but have not been able to substantiate this because of the paucity of available information. The relationship must have developed during Louis's childhood. One can imagine Charles sending his artistic son to study at the knee of Edward C. Moore, in the hope that Louis would one day become a designer at Tiffany & Co. or learn the rudiments of silversmithing. After all, Charles had learned *his* business skills while working in his father's store.

Moore established a system of artistic instruction and training for his apprentices which became known as the "Tiffany School". Drawing and modelling from natural objects were part of the curriculum. (Later Tiffany designers such as Paulding Farnham and John Curran received their training in this school.) Although it is not known precisely when Moore organized the school, it is likely that Louis Comfort Tiffany was one of his first pupils.

Throughout Louis Tiffany's life, he sketched directly from nature, in the same manner as Moore instructed his young protégés. According to Michael John Burlingham, Tiffany spent the summer of 1865, after he finished his studies at Eagleswood Military Academy, strolling the grounds around his father's summer house, Tiffany Hall, near the village of Irvington-on-Hudson, and sketching flowers.[8] After his studies with Moore, drawing from the actual flower would have been routine. This was an activity he pursued the whole of his artistic life. I propose that he began working with Moore as early as 1860, when he was twelve years old. Most artists begin drawing as soon as they can hold a writing instrument. Louis must have been sketching as a child, and it would have been natural for him to turn to Moore for instruction.

Edward Moore amassed a personal collection of books and objets d'art, as well as one for Tiffany & Co., before libraries and museums were available to the general public. He encouraged his designers to turn to these sources for inspiration. Among the volumes in the Tiffany & Co. archives are encyclopaedias on various topics such as plants, books on Japanese art and wallpaper, Persian art, photographs of flowers from nature, Hokusai's *Mangwa*, and Owen Jones's *The Grammar of Ornament*, which served as a guide for designers in the decorative arts throughout the 19th century after its publication in 1856. Moore's personal collection contained the Jones volume as well as Christopher Dresser's *Principles of Decorative Design*, some books on Persian and Arabic art, and many books on Japanese art. Moore's example may have inspired Louis Tiffany to put together a library of his own that also included Jones's *The Grammar of Ornament* as well as many books on flowers, plants, gardens, birds, butterflies, Arabian art, and Chinese pottery and porcelain. An analysis of the subject-matter of these three libraries makes it apparent that both Moore and Louis Tiffany were interested in material relevant to their designing specialities, especially books on Oriental and Persian art, plants, and current design pattern guides.

One can imagine Louis as a child browsing through the books at the Tiffany & Co. studio, and Moore instructing his young charge in art-history lessons or in the fine arts of the East. Moore used these books as source material for his designs but very rarely copied from them directly.[9] Instead, he would assimilate the material and transpose it into the Tiffany idiom.

Many of the etched and applied decorative elements in Tiffany & Co.'s Japanesque silver are based on illustrations in Hokusai's *Mangwa,* of which there are three volumes in the Tiffany archives. Moore did not copy these motifs; a spider or dragonfly may resemble examples in the *Mangwa,* but they are rendered in a Western manner, not in the original Oriental style. Moore never deviated from this policy. For the 1893 World's Columbian Exposition in Chicago, he instructed his designers to make an Indian bowl, based on a Pueblo water basket.[10] The repoussé decoration of Southwestern US flora is conceived in a three-dimensional manner, while the inlaid copper and niello patterning that decorates the surface is an abstraction of an Indian design. Again, Moore was looking at other sources but translating them into his own creative language.

Louis Tiffany also used his library as inspiration for his designs and, like Moore, never directly copied from the source material. The dragonfly was a motif that both designers incorporated onto their objects. Tiffany 3· reinterprets it on his lamps, superimposing the dragonfly over a stream or pond in the background, in much the same manner as Moore designed a dragonfly 2 skimming across the surface of water on a vase. Moore was striving for polychromatic effects in his dragonflies; the bodies and wings were made of several metals, such as silver, gold, copper, and Japanese alloys of shakudo and shibuichi. Tiffany uses varicolored glass to achieve a similar effect. The dragonflies on Tiffany's lamps and brooches are stiffer, almost as if the insect were pinned to a board, while Moore's example more closely resembles the insect in flight, with its body curved and wings slightly tapering. Although the dragonfly was a common Art Nouveau motif at the turn of the century, Tiffany may have selected it in homage to Moore.

Both Moore and Tiffany amassed large collections of art objects from the Near and Far East. Tiffany's collection included ancient art glass,

*Marginal numbers refer to color illustrations.

Japanese tsubas and inro, Japanese and Chinese paintings and prints, Oriental carpets, lacquer work and carvings, as well as American Indian basketry. He displayed his tsubas, or Japanese sword guards, in the smoking room at Laurelton Hall, his estate at Oyster Bay, Long Island, adorning the fireplace, door casings and lamps, as well as storing them in cabinets.[11] Moore also collected tsubas and it is believed that the decoration on these articles influenced the decorative motifs on his Japanesque silverware.

Located in the Tiffany archives is a photographic scrapbook of the firm's Union Square location and the Prince Street facility. One page depicts the silver design studio, illustrating the library and art collection, which includes a glass cabinet with American Indian baskets. In 1877 Moore also acquired on Tiffany & Co.'s behalf articles from the auction sale of items Christopher Dresser had collected in the Far East. Moore bought many of the lots for his own collection, although the precise objects are unknown.

The eventual disposition of both Moore's and Tiffany's libraries and collections was also similar: both were intent on benefiting future generations. Moore's library and collection were bequeathed to the Metropolitan Museum of Art. When he died in 1891, the books became part of the Museum's library while the objets d'art were displayed as a unit in a separate room. Eventually, as the Museum expanded, the collection was dispersed to appropriate departments.

Louis Tiffany assembled his collection for his own study as well as for his artists at Tiffany Studios to use for research. The collection was originally housed at Tiffany Studios in New York. It was then moved to Laurelton Hall, where it was presented to the Louis Comfort Tiffany Foundation in 1919 as a research facility for promising artists. It remained part of the Foundation until the contents of the house were sold at public auction in 1946.

Besides his early artistic instruction under Edward Moore, Tiffany enrolled in art classes while a student at Eagleswood Military Academy in Perth Amboy, New Jersey. Before attending Eagleswood, he had gone to the Flushing Boarding School on Long Island. His father sent him to Eagleswood for the 1862–63 academic year when he was 14, and he remained at the school three years. Doreen Bolger Burke maintains that it was here that Tiffany studied under the artist George Inness; and also that he may have met James Steele MacKaye, who introduced him to Oscar Wilde as well as offering him two interior decorating commissions.[12]

It has often been stated that Louis Tiffany was unhappy during his first year at Eagleswood. At first, he could not adapt to the rigors of a military academy, but he must have adjusted by the second year since he was listed among those who were not given any demerits for the next two years.[13]

All students, with the exception of the senior level, were given art instruction in drawing; the academy's brochure listed the course as ''Figure, Landscape, and Mechanical Drawing.''[14] Charles Tiffany, a thorough man in every aspect of his professional life, must have been aware of the art instruction at Eagleswood and the inherent advantage for his gifted son. Not only would Louis have the benefits of a strict education, but he would also be studying with artists in the field, especially George Inness. According to Burke, Eagleswood was a school to which many prominent Americans sent their sons, among them the journalist Parke Godwin; the writer and educator Mary Tyler Peabody Mann, widow of Horace Mann; Marcus Ward, governor of New Jersey; and William F. Havemeyer, mayor of New York City. The painters George Caleb Bingham and Christopher Pearse Cranch, and the famous photographer Matthew B. Brady also favored the school.[15] Frederick Law Olmsted, the landscape architect who is best known for his design of New York's Central Park, acted as an adviser to the school.[16]

Inness evidently moved to Perth Amboy in 1863, after Marcus Spring, one of the sponsors of the school, offered him a house in exchange for a painting. He remained there until 1867, two years after Tiffany left the Academy. Although Inness was not an official teacher at the school, Burke suggests that ''he probably offered at least informal instruction both to some of the more talented young men at the school and to some members of the community that surrounded it.''[17] She quotes Inness's son, George Jr.: ''While at Eagleswood there were many artists who congregated around my father, and he had some pupils. Louis C. Tiffany was one.''[18]

Inness did not give formal classes in art; instead, he would advise his students on how they could improve their work. His was a rather Socratic method, in which the instructor would raise questions about the good or bad points of a student's work, letting the student decide how to proceed. This is an ideal method for developing an artistic ''eye'', the ability to distinguish what is aesthetically good from what is mediocre. In *The Art of Louis Comfort Tiffany*, which is actually Tiffany's autobiography, Charles DeKay writes that ''Inness did not give instruction in painting; his way was to criticise or appreciate the work of a young artist from time to time . . . He set high ideals before the student. He was a colorist and as such could not fail to appeal to Tiffany.''[19] It was while studying with Inness that Tiffany developed an appreciation for the importance of color in art, a characteristic that would dominate his work.

Tiffany's years at Eagleswood Military Academy were fruitful. In his second year, he received an award for proficiency in drawing, an indication that he had learned his lessons well, and perhaps that his talents as an artist had been awakened under the guidance of Edward Moore before his attendance at the

The award Louis Comfort Tiffany won at his school, Eagleswood Academy, on July 1st, 1864, ''for Proficiency in Drawing.'' He was 16 years old at the time. *(Charles Hosmer Morse Museum of American Art, Winter Park, FL)*.

Academy. Charles Tiffany's decision to send his son to Eagleswood proved to be a wise one.

After Tiffany finished his formal schooling, it was time for him to travel and see at first hand the wonderful European masterpieces that had been available to him only in books. In the latter half of the 19th century, young people of means were expected to take a European tour after completion of their formal education. Edward Moore had traveled to Paris in 1855, ostensibly to see the latest European silverware at the Paris Exposition and sketch anything that caught his fancy. While there, he also visited the Louvre and the Luxembourg Museum, where he studied classical objects in silver and ceramics.[20]

It would have been natural for Moore to encourage young Tiffany to travel to see the European masterpieces. Besides, if Charles Tiffany had wanted to mould his son in his own image, he would no doubt have insisted that Louis work at Tiffany & Co. the summer after completing his studies at Eagleswood instead of allowing the boy to amuse himself sketching flowers. Why would he send his son to Europe if not to encourage his artistic talents?

In the autumn after leaving Eagleswood, Louis Tiffany traveled to Europe with his sister, Annie Olivia, and their aunt Lydia Young, widow of Charles Tiffany's first partner. They left on 1 November 1865, and visited England, Ireland, France, Italy and Sicily before returning on 21 March 1866.[21] Like Moore, Louis spent the majority of his time sketching. A sketchbook from this trip contains drawings and watercolors of flowers and the European landscape. Although the drawing is amateurish, Gary Reynolds identifies the following qualities that were to be evident in his later work: ''a sensitivity to color and form and a fascination with exotic, picturesque subjects.''[22] These are characteristics that were particularly marked in Tiffany's later enamels and jewelry.

The following summer he spent just as he had the previous one, wandering the fields near his father's summer house and drawing flowers. Back in New York that autumn, Louis entered formal art classes at the prestigious National Academy of Design. Although this institution was the accepted school which every striving young artist attended, it did not suit Louis's temperament. The course of study there was based on a formalized, academic approach to drawing. Students first began sketching from plaster casts. Draughtsmanship was stressed; color was secondary. It was not long before Tiffany realized that this type of training was not suitable to his talents. After studying with George Inness, he could not be satisfied with this approach to art instruction. Tiffany was a restless spirit, who wanted to follow his own instincts and not the dictates of others.

It may have been at this time that he began to frequent the studio of the painter Samuel Colman, who was to have the greatest impact on his artistic career and eventually became his traveling companion and business partner. Although there are no surviving records concerning their relationship, DeKay writes that Tiffany "was haunting the studios of . . . Samuel Colman, N.A."[23] It is likely that Tiffany visited Colman's studio in New York, not as a student but as an observer, and gradually assimilated Colman's style. Gary Reynolds noted many parallels in their styles and subject-matter from the late 1860s and early '70s. Both arranged their compositions in similar ways, including the duplication of several views of the Hudson River; and both emphasized identical color, light and atmosperic effects in their paintings.[24]

In 1868, Louis Tiffany set out for Europe again, this time to study with Léon Charles Adrien Bailly in Paris. He remained only a year, establishing his headquarters at Tiffany & Co.'s office. When he returned to New York, he set up a studio at the YMCA on 23rd Street and continued to paint in the style of the Hudson River painters, notably George Inness.

In the spring of 1870, Tiffany was traveling once more, but this time, instead of visiting European landmarks, he set out with Samuel Colman to explore North Africa. Tiffany's interest in the Near East may have been spurred on by the paintings of Léon Adolphe Auguste Belly, whose studio he had visited while studying in Paris. Although Tiffany did not actually take any classes with Belly, according to DeKay he admired the Frenchman's work and acknowledged that Belly was "a landscapist who traveled in northern Africa, Egypt, and Palestine."[25] Whether or not this was the impetus behind Tiffany's journey to the Near East, it is clear that he reveled there in the exotic nature of the landscape, the people and their customs.

Tiffany and Colman traveled throughout the Muslim world of Africa, from Egypt to Tangier, and then across to Spain. The vibrant colors and the subdued atmospheric light in these regions had a strong effect on Tiffany. Many years later, he said that

When first I had a chance to travel in the East and to paint where the people and the buildings also are clad in beautiful hues, the preeminence of color in the world was brought forcibly to my attention. I returned to New York wondering why we made so little use of our eyes, why we refrained so obstinately from taking advantage of color in our architecture and our clothing when Nature indicates its mastership, when, by its use under the rules of taste, we can extend our innocent pleasure and have more happiness in life.[26]

Tiffany was impressed by atmospheric colorations which had not been known to him heretofore. Hugh McKean, a painter who studied at Laurelton Hall, wrote that ''pure colors to a conservative painter are a forbidden world. All the colors we see in nature are grayed a little by the atmosphere.''[27] Bright, glaring colors were anathema to Tiffany, who preferred subdued colorations in his work, especially in his watercolors, where he chose combinations of opaque and transparent colors. He was also to use these color tones when he came to design enamelware and jewelry. He bypassed pure colored gemstones, such as rubies, emeralds or sapphires (except in certain instances to achieve coloristic effects), selecting instead moonstones, opals, jade, carnelian, or lapis lazuli, which provided colors more in keeping with the palette of his impressionistically rendered paintings.

Tiffany's canvases are imbued with the spirit of the Near East. These atmospheric hues and Byzantine motifs were to predominate in his work. Tiffany continued to travel even after his marriage to Mary Woodbridge Goddard on 15 May 1872, sometimes in the company of Samuel Colman. In 1908, he returned to North Africa, travelling in a yacht up the Nile.

Siegfried Bing, in his catalogue for the ''Exhibition of L'Art Nouveau'', held at the Grafton Galleries in Paris in 1899, described the Eastern impact on young Tiffany as follows:

What impressed the young artist and filled his heart with a transport of emotion never felt before, was the sight of the Byzantine basilicas, with their dazzling mosaics, wherein were synthesised all the essential laws and all the imaginable possibilities of the great art of decoration. Exploring the depths of a far-distant and glorious past with the aid of these venerable monuments, Tiffany dreamed a dream of Art for the Future.[28]

Never copying directly from these sources, Tiffany absorbed Eastern art and translated it into his own artistic language—as Moore had done in his designs for Tiffany silver. In Gertrude Speenburgh's view, ''No Occidental artist has worshipped more ardently at the shrine of Oriental art than did Louis C. Tiffany.''[29]

In 1879, Louis formed an association known as Louis C. Tiffany and Associated Artists, with the purpose of encouraging good taste in America, much as Edward W. Godwin, James Abbott McNeill Whistler, and Christopher Dresser had done in England. His initial partners in this endeavor were Samuel Colman; Lockwood de Forest, a painter and specialist in East Indian carvings and fabrics; and Candace Wheeler, director of her own organization specializing in needlework. Up to this period, interior decoration was based on heavily patterned design schemes. By introducing new color tonalities into decoration, as well as elements from design sources other than European, Associated Artists strove to establish a new standard of taste. Harmony was achieved through attention to detail; every item in the room was taken into consideration. Exotic motifs were incorporated onto objects produced in their own workshops, such as painted friezes, glass tiles, mosaic wall panels, lighting fixtures, wallpapers, embroidered wall hangings, carpets, and furniture.

One of Associated Artists' early commissions in 1880 was to decorate the library and Veterans' Room of the Seventh Regiment Armory in New York City. Armories were just beginning to emerge in the US in response to national security. They became the site of grand ceremonial proceedings, held in celebration of American history, largely in response to the recent Centennial celebration held in Philadelphia. Tiffany, in charge of the overall plan of the two rooms, conceived a design scheme based on military themes. Everything about the Veterans' Room proclaimed "military triumph:"[30] the oak wainscot which stood 10 feet high, the frieze which ran directly under the ceiling recounting the history of the world's wars, the columns which were partially wound with linked chains, the furniture that could have been at home in a medieval fortress, and the wrought-iron chandeliers. William Brownell described the room as "a decorative expression of the idea of the veteran."[31] Garance Aufaure recently referred to the Armory design as a "space in which Crusaders or the Knights of the Round Table would feel quite at home."[32]

Louis Tiffany is credited with designing the lighting fixtures and furniture for the Armory commission, which are prototypes of his later work. These items are embellished with Islamic wire-work and naturalistic motifs, both design elements he would incorporate into every facet of his later oeuvre, especially his jewelry and enamels. Nature, particularly flowers, played a dominant role in his work, as it did in much of 19th-century fine and decorative arts. In his famous essay, "Nature", written in 1836, Ralph Waldo Emerson maintained that "we find nature to be the circumstance which dwarfs every other circumstance, and judges like a god all men that come to her. . . . Nature is loved by what is best in us. It is loved as the city of God." Emerson's views were well known in America throughout the century, and it is likely that Tiffany was aware of them. In a speech at his birthday breakfast on 19 February 1916, he quoted Philip James Bailey, "Art is man's nature; nature is God's art."[33] In an address before the Rembrandt Club of Brooklyn in 1917, he expounded on the preeminence of color in nature, especially flowers, concluding that "Beauty is what Nature has lavished upon us as a Supreme Gift—it is all about us to see and use."[34] Plant life became a leading theme in Tiffany's work as early as the Armory commission. The armchairs he designed for the Veterans' Room are embellished with relief carvings of leaves on the arms and finials, a subtle detail on a heavy piece of furniture designed for a room of massive proportions. The leaves act to soften the overall heaviness of the chairs.

Nature was also emulated in Europe, due in large part to the writings of Owen Jones and Christopher Dresser. *The Grammar of Ornament* included a section, "Leaves and Flowers from Nature", while Dresser's *The Art of Decorative Design* included a chapter entitled "The Ministrations of Plants to Ornament." Both authors explain how a simple plant can be the source for inventive decorative designs.

The middle and latter part of the 19th century was also a period when Americans believed that their country was destined to span the land between the Atlantic and Pacific Oceans. Artists such as George Catlin lived among the Indian tribes, sketching their chieftains and their daily activities. Martin Johnson Heade traveled to Brazil to paint the indigenous hummingbirds and flowers. This was a time of extensive exploration, when exotica could be found within one's own land. It was in this pervasive atmosphere that Louis Comfort Tiffany was developing his artistic style.

The other dominant theme in Tiffany's work is historicism. The 19th century was characterized by revivalism, in which virtually every past era was invoked during some part of the century. Tiffany did not turn to such revivals as neo-classical or Renaissance, but rather to the Eastern influences absorbed during his travels. Filigree wire-work became an important motif, as seen on the Armory chandelier in the library, where heart-shaped motifs are reminiscent of Islamic wire-work. The theme is continued on the mantel candelabra which provided illumination for the painted stucco relief of an eagle swooping down on a dragon. Tiffany was to use similar configurations in his later jewelry made at Tiffany & Co., but instead of leaving spaces void, he would fill the area with plique-à-jour enameling.

The recent success of Louis C. Tiffany and Associated Artists prompted Charles Tiffany to invite his son to join the Board of Directors of Tiffany & Co. Accordingly, on 7 June 1881, when he was 33 years old, Louis Tiffany was elected a director on the Board of Trustees of Tiffany & Co. at their annual stockholders meeting.[35] His father was surely aware by this time that

The chandelier Tiffany designed to hang in the library of the Seventh Regiment Armory in New York City. Drawing upon exotic cultures for its inspiration, the chandelier incorporates heart-shaped motifs, influenced by Islamic wire-work. *(Historic American Building Survey, Seventh Regiment Fund, Inc.).*

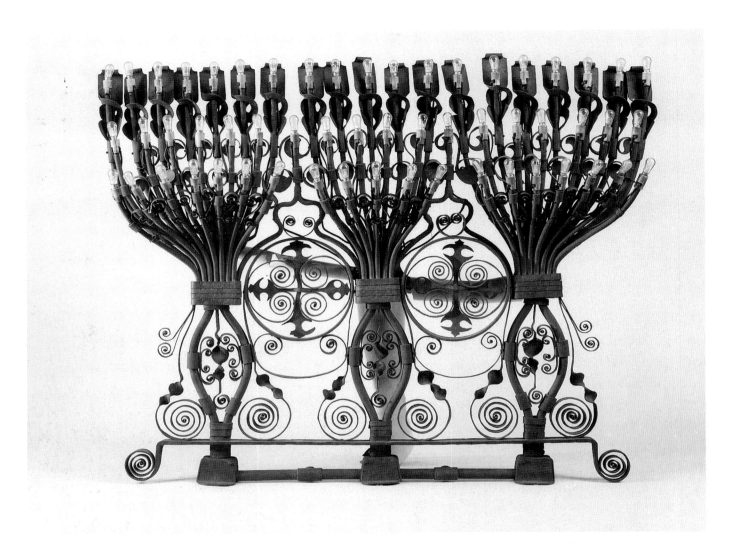

Spiral motifs on the mantel candelabra designed for the Seventh Regiment Armory commission in 1879–80. These elements were to appear again later in Tiffany's jewelry designs. *(Seventh Regiment Fund, Inc.)*.

Louis had no intention of formally joining the company, and was resigned to his son's wish to operate his own firm.

Louis C. Tiffany and Associated Artists dissolved their partnership in 1883, Candace Wheeler retaining the name "Associated Artists" for her own company. In 1885, Tiffany formed a new concern, known as the Tiffany Glass Company, which continued to accept interior decorating commissions. In 1890, he undertook a commission to decorate the new mansion of Louisine and Henry Osbourne Havemeyer at 1 East 66th St., New York. The Havemeyers, having amassed a splendid collection of Old Master and Impressionist paintings and decorative art objects, wanted to build a house that would be monumental on the exterior but give no outward indication of the treasures to be found within. Tiffany's influence was also evident on the façade, which was based on his own mansion at the corner of Madison Avenue and 72nd St., a building that was Romanesque in appearance.

Tiffany worked on this commission with his former business partner, Samuel Colman, who was also a personal friend of the Havemeyers. Tiffany's most memorable work in this house was the "flying" staircase in the picture gallery. Aside from its intrinsic value, this construction is worthy of note because it contained design elements that lay at the root of his jewelry creations, which began formally a decade later.

Aline Saarinen describes it in *The Proud Possessors*:

. . . the gallery became a topic of animated conversation by virtue of its "golden" or "flying" staircase. A narrow balcony with an alcove ran around the second story of the picture gallery. The spectacular staircase was suspended, like a necklace, from one side of the balcony to the other. A curved piece of cast iron formed the spine to which, without intermediate supports, the stair treads were attached. The sides of this astonishing construction, as well as the balcony

For the second-floor picture gallery in the Havemeyer house, which Tiffany decorated in 1892, he designed a special "flying" staircase that hung like a necklace from one side of the balcony to the other. *(Photograph courtesy of the Metropolitan Museum of Art).*

railing, were a spider web of gold filigree dotted with small crystal balls. The concept of a construction in space was revolutionary indeed for 1890, and its daring was dramatized by a crystal fringe on the center landing which tinkled from the slight motion when the staircase was used.[36]

Although this staircase was monumentally conceived, it was jewel-like in appearance, quite unlike the ponderous staircases in common use at the time, which dominated a room by their sheer mass. In contrast, Tiffany's suspended staircase transformed a utilitarian area of the house into a work of art.

The Havemeyers were patrons of music and sponsored Sunday afternoon concerts, held in a room specially built for that purpose. For this room, Tiffany designed chandeliers, inspired by Queen Anne's lace, that were light and airy in appearance. Plant and floral motifs were also evident on the furniture designed by Tiffany and Colman; however, instead of basing these motifs directly on nature as Tiffany had done with the chandeliers, they turned to Islamic art. The shallowly carved decoration is reminiscent of floral patterning from such

As early as the Havemeyer commission, Tiffany was creating objects based on floral motifs, such as these Queen Anne's lace chandeliers in the music room. *(Photograph courtesy of the Metropolitan Museum of Art).*

buildings as the Alhambra. This style derived from the aestheticism of the 1870s and was a look backward, instead of ahead towards the future naturalism signaled by the chandeliers.

Colman and Tiffany integrated Japanese, Chinese, Moorish, Viking, Celtic and Byzantine elements into the interior of the Havemeyer mansion, but it was the Byzantine influence that remained with Tiffany throughout his career, especially in his jewelry creations. A good example is the Byzantine-style pebble and glass chandelier, made up of concentric circle motifs, that originally hung in the Havemeyers' library. Pebbles were set within filigree framework in a manner similar to Tiffany's later jewelry designs when he substituted moonstones for pebbles, retaining similar configurations but using platinum or palladium to offset the pale color of the stones. Similar motifs are seen on a balustrade from the third-floor stairwell and a fireplace screen that incorporated opalescent glass within a filigree framework. At the entrance hall door, pebbles Louisine Havemeyer had collected from the beach were set within an intricate jewel-like filigree. This again foreshadows many features that appear in Tiffany's later jewelry creations.

6

The Byzantinesque motifs on the chandelier Tiffany designed for the Havemeyers' library appear again in the jewelry in which filigree mountings were created to encase gemstones. *(Photograph courtesy of the Metropolitan Museum of Art).*

The balustrade for the Havemeyer house had pale-toned opaline glass set into scrolling wire-work of gold-plated metal. On the interior of the entrance door to the house (opposite), beach pebbles collected by Louisine Havemeyer were mounted like jewels. *(University of Michigan School of Art and College of Architecture and Urban Planning, on extended loan to the University of Michigan Museum of Art).*

Byzantine-inspired elements are also evident in the ecclesiastical objects Tiffany exhibited in the chapel at the 1893 World's Columbian Exposition in Chicago, where he shared space with his father's firm, Tiffany & Co. Included among the articles he showed on this occasion were his first recorded use of gemstones. Hugh McKean characterized this display as "a proving ground for nearly everything he made later."[37] The tabernacle door from the altar was composed of a grille set with jade, amber, quartz pebbles, and mussel and abalone shells, very jewel-like in its conception. This door was admired many years after the installation of the chapel. *The Jewelers' Circular* illustrated it on the cover of the 23 February 1916 issue at a time when the chapel, which had been installed in a crypt at the Cathedral of St. John the Divine in New York, was closed for an indefinite period.

The original jeweled altar cross was mounted with white topazes, which, according to a review of the exposition in *The Decorator and Furnisher*, were "set so as to scintillate the light in every direction. This cross gives a good idea of their [*i.e.*, Tiffany Glass and Decorating Company] decorative church jewelry work."[38] Tiffany designed the cross with a radiating sun at the crossing,

For the chapel at the 1893 World's Columbian Exposition in Chicago, Tiffany designed these altar candlesticks set with glass jewels and quartz pebbles. *(Charles Hosmer Morse Museum of American Art, Winter Park, FL).*

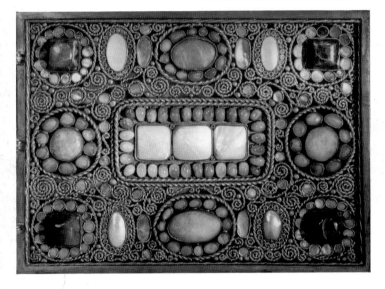

The tabernacle door was decorated with jade, amber, quartz pebbles, and mussel and abalone shells mounted in collet settings reminiscent of medieval goldsmiths' work. *(Charles Hosmer Morse Museum of American Art, Winter Park, FL).*

The original altar cross (opposite) was set with white topazes, chosen by Tiffany for their ability to reflect light. *(Reproduced from* The Decorator and Furnisher, *v. 23 (October 1893), p. 11).*

the rays emanating outward, reiterating the sparkling quality of the gemstones. The cross must have dazzled all who came to see the display.

On close examination, the above objects in Tiffany's display at the Columbian Exposition can be seen to derive from early goldsmiths' work, especially Ottonian books covers and crucifixes—a fact noted by Herwin Schaefer in his article, ''Tiffany's Fame in Europe.''[39] This attribution is apparent in both the conception and the execution of these objects. Stones are not faceted but cut *en cabochon* and mounted within closed or collet settings, a technique typical of medieval goldsmiths' work.

The original altar cross was lost while the chapel was in the Cathedral of St. John the Divine, but Tiffany replaced it after he installed the chapel at Laurelton Hall. It was designed along much simpler lines with opaline glass and glass buttons, mother of pearl, and iridescent favrile glass in a manner similar to the moonstone jewelry Tiffany was making during the same period. Even though it was fabricated more than twenty years after the Chicago exhibition, Tiffany recreated the cross in a fashion similar to the altar candlesticks. On the cross, glass beads are set into cames which are grooved lead

After Tiffany installed the chapel displayed at the 1893 Chicago exhibition in Laurelton Hall, he replaced the original altar cross with a simpler version (opposite) made of opaline and glass buttons, mother of pearl and favrile glass. *(Charles Hosmer Morse Museum of American Art, Winter Park, FL).*

A lantern on which Tiffany counterbalanced concentric circles and rectangular turtle back tiles.

bars in the shape of ribbons, used for holding together pieces of glass. On the candlesticks, chipped glass jewels and quartz pebbles are embedded into cames. On one of the candlesticks he used a rosette-shaped configuration of pebbles, which appeared again later on his jewelry. Although rosettes are common motifs in jewelry, it must be remembered that Louis Tiffany was not trained as a jewelry designer, and his use of such forms was not influenced by other jewelry forms but by those sources he had already drawn from when designing the lighting fixtures for the Armory commission, the Chicago chapel, and the interior of the Havemeyer house. This candlestick also used a filigree technique with twisted rope motif that was to appear later on Tiffany's jewelry.

Along with the candlesticks, Tiffany displayed a benediction candelabrum set with opalescent glass. The lower group of candles are set against Islamic trefoil cusped arches. This candelabrum, like the other articles in Tiffany's display, was in the neo-Byzantine style. In addition to the chapel, Tiffany had a separate exhibit of art objects, many set with gemstones and pearls, such as a chasuble made of velvet, gold thread and pearls; a mitre made up of needlework and enriched with gemstones; and an embroidery for the lectern frontal made of silks, jewels and gold.[40]

Even after the turn of the century, Tiffany continued to use motifs from Near Eastern art in his work. Concentric gilt-bronze rope twist decorative motifs soften the angularity of the horizontal bands on a chandelier, and also complement iridescent glass tiles on a lantern. In these examples, Tiffany was juxtaposing geometric shapes, using the concentric motifs prevalent in Islamic art—a version of filigree mounting that he later incorporated into his moonstone jewelry. He took this idea a step closer to his jewelry designs by setting polished pebbles within filigree decoration on the base of a lamp;[41] his jewelry often contained a central stone surrounded by an identical mounting.

In other examples, favrile glass was blown into a bronze framework composed of a variation of concentric circles. On a humidor the motif acts as a framework to hold the glass, as well as a decorative embellishment on the lid. The body of the humidor is free-form, whereas on a lamp of about the same period the glass is carefully encased within the framework in both the body and the feet. Bronze reeded strips cascade down to be joined at the feet with spirals. Again, Tiffany is counterbalancing opposing geometrical forms, using Near Eastern decorative motifs.

At this point, it seems appropriate to revisit the question of why Louis did not turn his artistic talents earlier in the direction of his father's principal business, jewelry. In an attempt at an answer, two related insights are appropriate. First of all, although Louis Tiffany did not formally pursue enamel work until 1898 and jewelry-making until after 1902, much of his oeuvre before

the turn of the century can be seen as relevant groundwork, culminating in his creation of jeweled vessels reminiscent of medieval goldsmiths' work. Secondly, an examination of his earlier production reveals that he had been developing and refining the aesthetic principles and technology he would eventually need to fully realize the jewelry and enamels he had in mind.

What he had in mind was, of course, quite different from those objects his father's designers were creating and which were receiving numerous awards toward the end of the 19th century. They may have been somewhat intimidating to him, so he simply decided that the time was not right to interfere with such success. This is particularly true of the jeweled splendors that Paulding Farnham had been creating for Tiffany & Co. and exhibiting at international exhibitions from 1889 to 1904. Examples included a corsage ornament set with over 2,000 diamonds, naturalistically rendered enameled orchids, and an iris brooch which measured $9\frac{1}{2}$ inches in height.[42] These items were so extravagant that no other American firm could come near to rivaling their magnificence. In concept, they were closer to French jewelry, a fact Henri Vever commented upon in his review of the Tiffany display at Chicago in 1893 when he wrote that "one would have been tempted to believe that they [the jewels] were made in Paris."[43]

Louis's conception of jewelry was at odds with the pieces being made at Tiffany & Co. To him, color was paramount; gemstones were to be selected for their polychromatic effects, not for their monetary value. He also preferred an impressionistic rendering of the subject, whereas Farnham was more strictly classical in his conception, in keeping with traditional Tiffany & Co. jewelry. When Farnham turned to nature for inspiration, flowers and birds were copied directly from specimens brought to the design studio for study. Louis Tiffany also modeled from nature but was not afraid to extend its power and beauty to create novel shapes and colors.

In view of the above, Louis Tiffany's approach towards a fuller association with Tiffany & Co. clearly had to be a gradual one. Initially, he exhibited his stained glass windows, favrile glass, and lamps at international exhibitions as part of the Tiffany & Co. display. However, as these items were not part of Tiffany & Co.'s stock in trade, they were not competing with the products of his father's firm. He also took advantage of the opportunity to collaborate with Paulding Farnham on a few selected items exhibited in the 1900 Exposition Universelle in Paris.

Ultimately, he waited for the opportune moment after his father's death in 1902 to make his move. Louis was an obedient son who would not want to engender any criticism from his father. Both were strong men, but one was the father and the other the son.

2

The Early Enamels

Louis Comfort Tiffany sought to unite the various divisions of his growing organization under one direction. His idea of a great workshop, with himself as head, resembles the famous Renaissance and Baroque ateliers in which artists such as Titian and Rubens maintained a staff of apprentices and assistants who carried out their orders. But instead of focusing on only one area, painting, Tiffany had grander designs. He wanted to combine all aspects of the decorative arts within one management and realize his artistic vision in each division. Siegfried Bing summed up his philosophy:

Tiffany saw only one means of effecting this perfect union between the various branches of industry: the establishment of a large factory, a vast central workshop that would consolidate under one roof an army of craftsmen representing every relevant technique: glassmakers and stone setters, silversmiths, embroiderers and weavers, casemakers and carvers, gilders, jewelers, cabinetmakers—all working to give shape to the carefully planned concepts of a group of directing artists, themselves united by a common current of ideas.[1]

Tiffany's organization was loosely based on similar establishments in England, such as the Guild of Handicraft organized by C. R. Ashbee, and Morris and Company established by William Morris. Whereas the ideal of creating well-designed objects was common to both Tiffany and his English counterparts, the English organizations were a conglomerate of many artistic individuals with, idealistically speaking, no distinction between employer and employees, whereas Tiffany's was run on a vertical principle, with himself as head, making all the decisions, and his staff creating the objects he envisioned.

Until the 1890s, Tiffany's artistic repertoire centered on painting, ornamental and ecclesiastical windows, and interior decorating commissions. Beginning about 1893, he turned his efforts to the design and creation of small utilitarian objects in a variety of new media, such as blown glass, metals, enamels, pottery and jewelry. This period of his artistic activity lasted for over a decade and, according to Martin Eidelberg, "was perhaps the most fertile portion of Tiffany's career and the period in which Tiffany gained his international fame."[2]

According to a chronology of Tiffany's life in *Masterworks of Louis Comfort Tiffany*, it was in 1892 that he formed the Tiffany Glass & Decorating Company in Corona, Long Island. (It was later renamed Tiffany Studios.) The original set-up included the establishment of a glass furnace facility that was to play a significant role in Tiffany's artistic endeavors. In about 1893, he splintered the glass-making operation off from Tiffany Glass & Decorating Company, and divided it into two business entities, the Stourbridge Glass Co. and the Allied Arts Company. The former, which would become Tiffany Furnaces in 1902, consolidated the manufacture of Louis Tiffany's glassware under the direction of Arthur J. Nash, an experienced glassmaker from Stourbridge, England. The Allied Arts Company provided manufacturing support for all other facets of Tiffany's oeuvre.[3]

Although Tiffany had definite ideas about the objects he was creating, he did not possess the technical background necessary to implement his designs. He therefore hired experts who could help him realize his creations. For example, Dr. Parker McIlhinney, a chemist, was brought into the organization to make scientific evaluations of the chemical properties of glass and to experiment with new mixtures. Tiffany worked closely with McIlhinney, who formulated the chemicals, and with Nash, who crafted the glassware.

The concept of scientists and craftsmen working together with a designer was not novel to Tiffany. Beginning in the 1870s, Edward C. Moore had maintained a chemical division at Tiffany & Co.'s silver workshop where scientists re-created the Japanese alloys of shakudo and shibuichi and, in the 1880s, perfected the various enamels that decorated the surface of their silver. It is likely that Tiffany was patterning his glass workshop after Moore's example. Just as Moore would design a particular object and instruct his chemists to create the appropriate metals for the silversmiths to use in their production, Tiffany would make a sketch of his idea, and his chemist and glassmaker would bring it to fruition.

Tiffany was an artist who thirsted for fresh and exciting departures. It is not surprising that he should have chosen enameling on metals as a new venture. Enamelware, like glass, must be heated in a furnace at a high temperature in order to realize the artistic creation. Hugh McKean has suggested that "Anyone with a glass furnace and a driving urge to try new techniques would be fascinated with enamels."[4] Thus Tiffany's interest in enameling on metal may well have been a natural outgrowth of his work with glass. However valid this point of view, it focuses rather narrowly on the technology of enameling. A broader analysis of Tiffany's life and work points to the driving force behind his love affair with enamels. Lewis Day provides an enlightening hint: "Enamel is inseparable from glass-working. In it the glass-worker comes to the help of the goldsmith, and gives him colour beyond the range of the available metals . . ."[5] Color: a lifetime obsession of Tiffany's, evident throughout his career no matter what medium he chose for his creativity. To Tiffany, color was paramount, and the infinite variety of colors obtainable through enameling would enable him to create objects with hues not available in his pottery or glass work. Thus a combination of the availability of furnaces and Tiffany's strong desire to capture the essence of color made enameling inevitable. It was not a consequence of his glassmaking but another step towards a fuller expression of his interest in color.

In 1898, Tiffany undertook his first experiments with enameling on metals at the Stourbridge Glass Co. facility. In the beginning of this new enterprise, he relied on his glassware staff to make the necessary chemicals. McIlhinney created the chemicals for the new department, serving in the same capacity as in the glassware division. Within a short time, Tiffany hired additional staff specialized in this area, among them Alice Gouvy and Julia Munson who, according to Himilce Novas, "was engaged to help him work out formulas and designs."[6] The department was originally set up in a small laboratory in Tiffany's mansion at 72nd Street and Madison Avenue; eventually it was moved to 23rd Street and then, in 1903, to the glass shop at Corona.[7]

Patricia Gay was put in charge of the newly formed department.[8] She was the daughter of the painter Edward Gay and, according to Robert Koch, she and her brother Duncan Gay both worked for Tiffany, although he does not say in what capacity Duncan was employed.[9] She remained part of Tiffany's operation until World War I. At that time she enlisted in the Women's Camouflage Corps; later, she returned to Tiffany Furnaces and worked there from 1921 to 1928.[10]

Julia Munson, born in New Jersey in 1875, was the daughter of a physician. She showed an early bent for art, and was a voracious reader of William Morris's writing. At the age of 23 she began her apprenticeship under Louis Tiffany, entering his employment just after art school.[11] Many sources claim that she created Louis Tiffany's wonderful enamels at their inception in 1898; however, it is unlikely that he would have enlisted a 23-year-old novice to experiment with his latest enterprise. She worked under the direction of Patricia Gay until she showed sufficient aptitude to be entrusted with the creation of important articles for Tiffany, who was known as a strict taskmaster. As Novas suggested, she was hired to work out formulas and designs under the capable direction of Dr. McIlhinney and Patricia Gay.

The art of enameling is a relatively simple procedure, as described by Mrs. Nelson Dawson in her book, *Enamels*. "Enamel is a vitreous paste, opaque or translucent, coloured or quite plain, which is fused by heat on to a metal ground, and its proper place is in company with, and for the enrichment in colour of, the finer work in metal, chiefly in gold, silver, or copper."[12] It also adheres to iron and fine bronze. Enamel is composed of flint or silica with additions of lead, soda or potash, which has been reduced to a fine powder. (The addition of lead oxides makes the enamel more refractive of light, more elastic, and enables the mixture to adhere to the metal.) It is spread onto the surface of metal in a thin layer which is then heated, either in a kiln or over an open flame, to a temperature between 1,500 and 1,800 deg. Fahrenheit.

The foundation of enamel is a clear flux, or frit, colored by the addition of various metallic oxides. At the time when Louis Comfort Tiffany was engaged in enameling, oxides added to flux produced the following colors: oxide of tin, opaque white; iron, sea green and yellow; cobalt, royal blue; copper, turquoise blue; manganese, violet; silver and antimony, yellow; gold, crimson; chromium, green; uranium, fine yellow; and iridium, steel grey and black.[13]

Enameling on metals is an ancient art, dating as far back as the 13th century BC. Its purpose is to create a design or colored area contained within a delineated space. Since enameling was thought to "run" under high heat, it was necessary to contain the glass paste within a specific design through several methods. In cloisonné enameling, cells or cloisons are formed into walls or partitions, usually not more than 1/50th of an inch high, which are soldered onto the base-plate. Powdered enamel is placed into the spaces enclosed by the walls and the object is heated. The enamel spreads to cover the entire area within the cloisons. Usually, a second coat is applied to offset any irregularities.

In champlevé enameling, the areas to be enameled are carved out of the metal, leaving walls between the areas which perform the same function as cloisons. Colored enamel is then placed into the dug-out areas and the piece is fired. A modified version of this technique, known as *basse-taille*, requires that the ground be chased, carved, engraved or stamped to varying levels. When heated, the colors, depending upon their depth, are a different shade.

In Limoges enameling, named for the area in France where the technique was developed, the colors are applied to the surface of metal in a manner similar to painting, without walls or cells to confine the colors. In *en ronde bosse*, the enameled colors are applied onto an irregular base, usually a repoussé chased body. Due to the excessive dripping that may occur, up to ten firings are required.

These enameling techniques remained unchanged from the 16th to the late 19th century, when, in the Art Nouveau and Arts and Crafts movements, there was a resurgence in the art of enameling on metal. Most enamelers in this period preferred to follow the more traditional cloisonné and champlevé techniques, but it was Alexander Fisher in England who disproved the myth that enamel must be retained within constricting partitions. He perfected what he called "painted enamels", achieved through layering translucent enamels. His technique was popularized through his teachings and a series of articles, "The Art of Enamelling Upon Metal", that appeared in *The Studio* from 1901 through 1905, and in 1906 was published in book form.[14]

It is not known whether Louis Comfort Tiffany was aware of Fisher's teachings (the articles were published three years after he embarked on enameling), but of all the enamelers working in the 1890s, Fisher promoted a technique that was closest to the one Tiffany used. Both preferred enameling directly onto metal without using walls or cloisons. Fisher employed this technique to achieve pictorial depth and true colorations, as opposed to the dull colors in Limoges enameling. Like Fisher, Tiffany strove for a deeper range of colors, but unlike his English counterpart he took chemical experimentation a step further to achieve translucency, as in his favrile glass. As a colorist, Tiffany continued throughout his artistic life to stretch beyond the parameters of normal color tonalities in order to achieve hues that only nature could produce. Flowers, which had dominated his designs before he began his work with enamels, now took over as his major source of inspiration.

We know that both Fisher and Tiffany were able to accomplish their objectives by using similar techniques. However, no records have survived from Tiffany's enameling workshop that define the precise process he prescribed for his enamels. Thus, we have only the description provided in Fisher's article to help us gain an insight into how Tiffany may have mastered the painterly technique.

Fisher sought to disprove the theory that

enamel would fly off the metal [if painted onto the metal without the use of walls] . . . But, with due care and experience, there is no danger of such an event occurring. There are several conditions which successful enamelling demands . . . use hard enamels, and pure or almost pure metals, and pure water . . . Further, great cleanliness must be exercised: clean metals, clean tools and brushes, clean saucers, pots and planches—a clean furnace, and above all, clean, freshly ground enamels. Painted enamels are generally done upon copper. And for this purpose thin copper is the best . . . it may be necessary to anneal it several times—it is cleaned by being placed in a glazed porcelain bath containing a mixture of sulphuric acid and water, in the proportion of 1 to 20 parts. Then it is washed in water, and afterwards it is either dipped into strong aqua fortis, plunged into water to wash the acid off, and dried in warm oak sawdust; or it is rubbed bright with pumice powder and whiting. Thus, having obtained a clean piece of metal, the first layer of enamel is placed on the underneath side by means of a palette knife, a brush or spatula, and water. The water is dried out of it by blotting paper. It is then turned over, and the design having been drawn on the copper, this is filled in with the various enamels suitable to the design. After that it is fired and worked on either by heightening parts with white or foil, which are glazed with clear enamels, or the first coat of different enamels is amplified, varied, darkened or modified, as the case may be, by other layers and gradations of enamel. Thus by very careful manipulation any degree of variety in strength, in brilliancy of lustre, or depth of colour can be obtained.[15]

Tiffany preferred copper as the base for his enamels for much the same reason that Henry Cunynghame suggested in his book, *European Enamels*, "For larger work, humble but useful copper is employed in thin sheets. This metal shows only poorly through enamels; but beautiful subdued tones can be got from it, and for decorative work its sober, solid hues are most valuable."[16] The metal itself reacted with the enamels to form unpredictable colors, an effect that would have more than pleased Tiffany.

The process of forming copper vessels is similar to raising a piece of silver holloware. A piece of copper, cut suitably to accommodate the intended object, is hammered over an anvil until it is formed into the desired shape. The end product is seamless and can then be decorated in a variety of techniques. Many of Tiffany's enamel objects are embellished with repoussé chasing, a term that literally means "repulsed" or "pushed back" to create a design in relief. First, the area to be worked must be bumped out. This is done with the use of a snarling iron in which one end is secured into a vise and the other inserted into the vessel. The silversmith then taps lightly on the snarling iron close to the vise. The vibrations are transferred to the metal, forcing the sides to stretch. Next, the vessel is filled with pitch which provides a foundation for the chaser to push back the metal with his punches. Working on the outside, the chaser creates the desired design from the artist's rough sketch.

Tiffany, like Fisher, used gold leaf or "paillons" as an undercoating on many of his enamels.[17] Cunynghame describes the technique: "The copper is first covered with a coating of enamel, which is melted on in the furnace. Then leaf-gold or leaf-silver is put upon it, and fired till it adheres to the coating of melted enamel on which it has been placed. Upon the top of the leaf transparent enamel is now placed so as to give the effect of enamel upon gold. Thus at a small price the effect of enamel upon gold is produced."[18]

After experimenting for two years, Tiffany included selected pieces of enamelware among the items he displayed at major international exhibitions, beginning with the 1900 Exposition Universelle in Paris. He considered these items "sculpture in utilitarian forms", although he did advertise them for sale in the *Art Interchange* in 1903, and in the 1904 Tiffany & Co. *Blue Book*.[19] He continued to offer them in the *Blue Books* through 1914.

All of Tiffany's enamels bear an incised mark with either his initials or his name in facsimile. According to the advertisement in the *Art Interchange*, "The large pieces all bear the name Louis C. Tiffany in full; the smaller, the initials L.C.T."[20] With the exception of a relatively small number of

Alice Gouvy and L. A. Palmie (see p. 48) executed many nature studies for Tiffany's enamel department which served as reference for his enamels on copper. This drawing of a corn flower was signed by Palmie and dated June 1902. *(Collection of Paula and Howard Ellman)*.

pieces that have special marks, most are inscribed with a number, preceded with the initials SG or EL. There is strong evidence that these two markings represent important distinctions between the corresponding sets of enamels.

I believe that SG stands for Stourbridge Glass Co., Tiffany's enamelware division. I base this opinion on analysis of stamps from several nature studies.

On a watercolor sketch for cornflowers, "Tiffany Furnaces" is stamped along with "Enamel Dept S.G. Co." The latter mark has been repeated on the paper label. These objects would date from the inception of the department in 1898 to 1902, the date when Stourbridge Glass Co. was absorbed into Tiffany Furnaces. There are several of Tiffany's enamels with what looks like an SC mark on the underside. The examples I have seen all fall within specific groups in the SG series. My conclusion is that the "C" is just an unfinished "G" (the same holds true for a few pieces in the other set, which have FL marks that should rather be EL). One can speculate on several ways these imperfections might have come about.

The numbering system in both series runs sequentially, beginning with number 1. The numbers in the SG series continue to 350, while the EL series goes up to 300. In addition, Tiffany made about 100 special items with other numbering codes. Thus, a fair estimate of his total enamelware production is 750 pieces over nine years, a rather small number considering his production in other areas.

Tiffany retained 90 of his enamels for his own collection, housed at Laurelton Hall.[21] In addition to these, in 1925 he presented on loan to the Metropolitan Museum of Art fifteen pieces that had also been part of his own collection. A simple calculation reveals that Tiffany kept almost 15 per cent of his total output in enamelware. If he intended to produce these items for commercial sale, why would he keep so many pieces for himself? I strongly believe that Tiffany considered this department a very special section of his workshop. His enamelware was made outside his normal production; it was never intended for commercial consumption in a mass market. He considered his enameled objects an art form, took personal care with the design of each piece, and made sure that they were executed precisely to his specifications. The Tiffany & Co. *Blue Book* of 1904 clearly states that the enamels were "Made under the personal supervision of Mr. Louis C. Tiffany . . . Tiffany Enamel is singularly unique and as distinctive in character as the Tiffany Favrile Glass."[22]

Tiffany's enamelware department was a very small part of his organization and the objects produced, although offered for sale, were made experimentally, to create unusual forms and color tonalities that he could not reproduce in his other media. Samuel Howe, a Tiffany employee, wrote in *The*

Craftsman that "experiments are now making, under the direction of Mr. Louis C. Tiffany, in his studio at Corona, Long Island, with the purpose of doing for enamel what has already been accomplished for glass."[23] Howe uses the explicit word "experiments" to describe Tiffany's foray into this new medium, a term also used by Henry Belknap in the same publication the following year, "Mr. Louis C. Tiffany has, for some years, been carrying on elaborate experiments in enamels."[24]

Tiffany created a variety of enamelware vessels, including vases, boxes, bowls, covered bowls, trays, pin trays, plaques, and desk accessories such as a paperweight, letter rack, stamp box, ink well, and a pin cushion (only one of each of the last five items is known). The Tiffany & Co. *Blue Book* describes these items as "relief and repoussée bodies, both with and without iridescent lustre. In the placing of translucent colors, one over another, effects are obtained by fire-art, similar to those in Favrile Glass."[25]

When Tiffany first began experimenting with enamels, he was interested in all aspects of the design, including form, surface treatment and color tonalities.[26] The early objects tended to be enclosed, either bowl- or urn-shaped. I believe the objects marked with SG are his first attempts in this new area. Within the SG series, Tiffany's enamelware can be divided into several distinct groups, based on specific parameters. He seems to have explored various design aspects until he was satisfied with the results, and only then would he move on to the next area. He did this, not in a haphazard manner, but most methodically. His enamelware evolved from the rounded to the cylindrical shape back to the rounded form, never copying the exact form on which he had previously worked.

Before I proceed with a more detailed analysis of the various SG groups, it is appropriate to introduce briefly Alice Gouvy and L. A. Palmie, who collaborated extensively with Tiffany in this phase. We know, as mentioned before, that Gouvy was in the department when it opened in 1898; it is not known when Palmie was first employed. These artists signed many of the drawings used to guide the production of Tiffany's enamels.

The drawings were used either as direct blueprints for specific objects, or as references for evolving decorative motifs eventually incorporated into object designs. In either case, drawings represent valuable aids for piecing together a coherent picture from the relatively small number of enamels known to exist today. They are particularly important because formal records of experiments on the chemistry, glassmaking, and other enameling technologies, carried out at Tiffany's direction by his trusted and capable technical assistants, are conspicuously missing.

9. Tiffany often depicted ferns on his enamel-on-copper objects. Although the foot of this vase is finished with a gold band, the lip follows the line of the fern fronds, with spaces in between to suggest the background. *(Charles Hosmer Morse Museum of American Art, Winter Park, FL).*

0. Three enamel-on-copper
vessels showing different aspects
of Tiffany's work in this field,
from the tall vase format to two
types of covered boxes, one
organically conceived and the
other a traditional shape. *(Center
vase, Metropolitan Museum of
Art, Gift of William D. and Rose
D. Barker, 1981).*

1. Another fern vase, raised from
a single piece of copper and the
fronds created in repoussé. The
coloring suggests the watery
environment in which the fern
grows. *(Collection of Paula and
Howard Ellman).*

12. In this vase, Tiffany depicted a
pepper plant growing downward,
its vines partially covering the
mouth and making it difficult
actually to use the piece. *(The
Museum of Modern Art, New
York, Joseph H. Heil Fund).*

13. The jack-in-the-pulpit motif used on the unusual vase below is rendered more like a piece of sculpture than a utilitarian object. *(Private collection).*

14, 15. The decorated vase at far right is one of the first known objects designed by Tiffany in enamel on copper and is dated 1898, whereas the bowl in the form of a tomato, with repoussé decoration of tomatoes in various stages of ripening *(Los Angeles County Museum of Art, gift of Mr. H. E. Rose)*, is in his mature naturalistic style.

16-18. Tiffany's use of natural motifs in his enamelwork extended to all the forms he created: here a particularly subtle vase with maple leaf patterns and seeds *(Charles Hosmer Morse Museum of American Art, Winter Park, FL)*; a vase with fuchsia blossoms, leaves and branches in repoussé; and a covered box with an apple motif *(Metropolitan Museum of Art, Gift of the Louis Comfort Tiffany Foundation, 1951).*

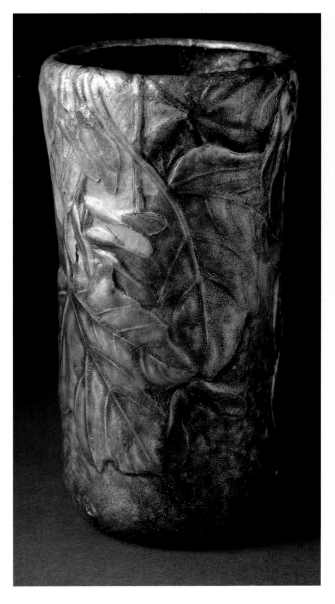

19. An enamel-on copper box on which iridized grape vines with leaves and fruit grow from the lid to the body. *(Private collection).*

20, 21. The covered boxes and enameled vases below were included in the gift of the Louis Comfort Tiffany Foundation to the Metropolitan Museum of Art in 1951.

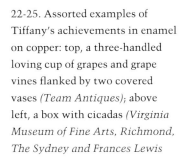

22-25. Assorted examples of
Tiffany's achievements in enamel
on copper: top, a three-handled
loving cup of grapes and grape
vines flanked by two covered
vases *(Team Antiques)*; above
left, a box with cicadas *(Virginia
Museum of Fine Arts, Richmond,
The Sydney and Frances Lewis*

Art Nouveau Fund); above, a
bowl with violets in repoussé
*(Metropolitan Museum of Art,
Gift of Louis Comfort Tiffany
Foundation, 1951)*; left, a stamp-
box in the shape of a rhinoceros
beetle, made between 1900 and
1902. *(Primavera Gallery).*

26. The pin cushion below has nasturtiums surrounding the fabric which simulates a garden environment. *(The Chrysler Museum, Norfolk, VA, Gift of Walter P. Chrysler, Jr.).*

27. Tiffany created a number of plaques in the medium of enamel on copper; this one depicts an assortment of sea motifs, including seaweed and oyster and mussel shells. *(Private collection).*

28. Tiffany designed covered boxes in the form of the fruit depicted, as he had done in the case of bowls; those shown above are a ripening raspberry and an eggplant. *(Private collection).*

29. This sculptural enameled letter-rack is composed of a marshy environment with jack-in-the-pulpits, reeds and a frog. *(Virginia Museum of Fine Arts, Richmond, The Sydney and Frances Lewis Art Nouveau Fund).*

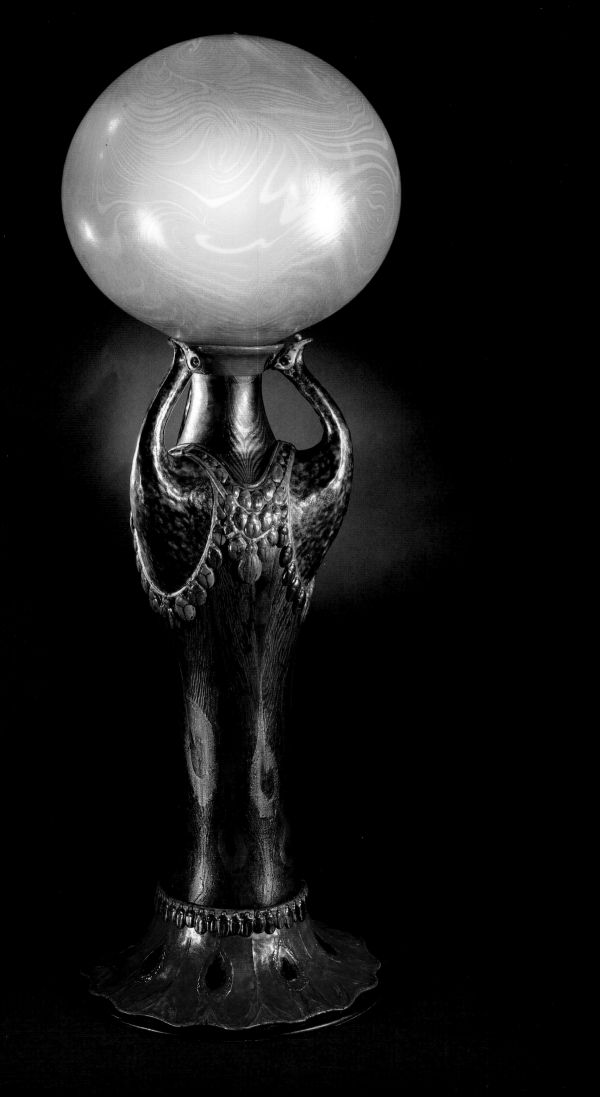

All extant drawings from Tiffany's enamelware department have been given a number, which usually appears on a paper label applied to the lower left-hand corner (some of these labels have since been removed). The numbering system for these drawings does not run in a straight chronological sequence as it does for the enamels themselves. Instead, it is structured into an alphabetical sequence, keyed to the initials of the plants represented in the designs. The first known sketch, number 4, is an arcerbia plant. Numbers continue up to 232, which appears on a sketch for violets.

Several of the sketches, signed by Gouvy and dating to 1900 and 1901, have been stamped "Tiffany Furnaces." Since Stourbridge Glass Co. was not absorbed into Tiffany Furnaces until 1902, I believe that at the time the drawings were organized and the labels attached, "Tiffany Furnaces" was also stamped onto the drawings. This stamp can be seen to be much darker than the other markings, which leads me to speculate that when Tiffany Furnaces took over Stourbridge Glass Co., all supplementary materials were so marked in order to identify them as belonging to the newly formed organization. An interesting and useful insight emerges from a critical study of known nature sketches signed by Alice Gouvy and by L.A. Palmie. Comparing these sketches to one another and to known enamels in the SG and EL series, one can see that these two sets of drawings are stylistically different: Gouvy's align themselves clearly with SG enamels, while Palmie's do so with EL pieces.[27]

All available evidence suggests that Tiffany started producing enamels in both the SG and EL series in 1898. For clarity, since these two series have distinct characteristics, I shall discuss them sequentially, starting with objects in the SG series. The first known piece in this series, a vase, bears the number 35 and would date to 1898. Its surface has been decorated in repoussé with red and yellow seed pods and leaves with dark brown branches over a maroon background. The lip is traditionally rendered with a simple gold band that picks up the colorations in the vase but abruptly cuts off the design. This is indicative of an early design but a detail that Tiffany modified as he continued to work in this medium. Although this vase was designed at an early date in the development of his enamelware department, Tiffany retained it and exhibited it in the 1902 Turin World's Fair.[28] Most of the enamel objects Tiffany displayed at the international fairs were not made in the year the exhibition took place. Rather, he seems to have saved his favorite pieces and, when the opportunity arose, contributed selected examples from his stock on hand.

The SG numbers from 40 to about 65 are all rounded forms in the shape of bowls, their surface in repoussé with a variety of plant motifs. On these vessels, enamel was applied in thin, even layers. The piece was then placed in a temperature-controlled furnace that evenly heated the object. To achieve an

14

Watercolor sketch of an arcerbia plant, executed shortly after the Stourbridge Glass Co. was absorbed into Tiffany Furnaces. *(Collection of Paula and Howard Ellman).*

30. This peacock lamp was created by Tiffany for Charles Gould. Three enameled peacock heads support the blown-glass shade. Necklaces with scarabs are suspended from each peacock and joined to the next to form a breastplate. *(Virginia Museum of Fine Arts, Gift of the Sydney and Frances Lewis Foundation).*

This drawing of a tomato plant, signed by Alice C. Gouvy, was used as a source for Tiffany's enamel-on-copper tomato bowl (Ill. 15). *(Charles Hosmer Morse Museum of American Art, Winter Park, FL)*.

Two enamel bowls showing the growth pattern of plants: a Virginia Creeper *(The Chrysler Museum, Norfolk, VA, Gift of Walter Chrysler, Jr.)* and an apple.

iridized effect, tin chloride was mixed with water or alcohol and sprayed on the enameled object, which was then placed back in the furnace for reheating. Hugh Weir, in his interview with Louis Tiffany in 1925, commented on this technique as it applied to glass, explaining that iridescence "may be accomplished by placing a sheet of plain glass in a properly heated oven and introducing various acid fumes."[29] Whether the fumes were sprayed on before or during firing, the result was the same. Tiffany was striving to duplicate in his enamelware the iridescence he had achieved in his glassware.

Tiffany incorporated recognizable plants on the surface of those pieces marked SG. He carefully chose the shape of each vessel to conform to the plant on the surface, thus achieving harmony between form and design. For example, if a plant is tall, it will appear only on tall vases, never on a rounded, squat form. Vines appear on both cylindrical and rounded forms. In the case of a flower container with a Virginia Creeper, the leaves spread over the surface of the vessel, leaving background spaces void, as plants do when they grow on a wall. The vine on the flower container continues from the body up to the grid, which has been flat chased to give the appearance of a real plant. This piece is numbered 43 and is the first known example in Tiffany's large bowl series.

Beginning with number 44, bowls are formed in the shape of the fruit depicted, such as plums, apples and tomatoes. A bowl in the collection of the Metropolitan Museum of Art[30] is shaped like a plum, created by repoussé on the surface. To enhance the "plumness" of the design, the enamel has been thinly applied to give coloristic depth to the fruit. Just as on a real plum, the color is not uniformly blue, but comprises a variety of shades.

A large tomato-shaped bowl was created by the same repoussé technique. The background of the design is a reddish color to simulate the fruit, and tomatoes and leaves wind around the surface in a manner similar to their growth pattern. The bowl replicates the shape of the tomato even to the ribbing detail close to the stem area. On all of Tiffany's bowls from this group, the metal is curved under the lip to give a more substantial feeling to the vessel. 15

The color of a tomato is also rendered realistically in various stages of ripening. Several tomatoes are slowly ripening and have been enameled with tones of red, yellow and green, evident on the watercolor sketch for the tomato bowl. One tomato is still green while another is fully developed, ready to be picked. The drawing is signed by A.C. Gouvy and dated 13 September 190? (the year date has been obliterated). A similar drawing of peppers and a pumpkin vine exist, also sketched by A.C. Gouvy.[31] The evidence of additional drawings would indicate that there are several more bowls in this series. In fact, the tomato-shaped bowl is number 61 and the next group begins about 70, suggesting that there were approximately thirty objects designed in the large bowl series.[32]

After his experiments with the bowl-shape, Tiffany turned to tall cylindrical vessels with plant forms in repoussé that grow either upwards or downwards; this series begins with number 72, and continues to 115 (*i.e.*, over 40 pieces). The first example is a vase in the collection of the Metropolitan Museum of Art. The surface is a corn plant in repoussé, enameled green and yellow. Because of its size, 14¾ inches in height, the ear of corn could be reproduced in its entirety. The lip on this vase was finished with a gold band, reiterated on the base. Since raising a tall slender shape would be very difficult, this example was not raised in the normal manner. Instead, the main body was formed by rolling a sheet of copper around a sleeve or cylinder, soldering the vertical seam and attaching the foot, also by soldering. Enameling the interior and exterior of the vase conceals any visible seams. Tiffany created several other examples in an identical shape, decorated with plant forms, such as a vase with irises that he displayed at the 1906 Salon of the Société des Artistes Français in Paris.[33]

The next known example from this series, number 80, was formed in the same manner as the previous one. However, instead of the lip's being finished with a corresponding gold band, the rim undulates in accordance with the fern fronds depicted. Tiffany created another vase with the same motif, but instead of alternating the fronds with the background, the rim is made up only of the plant motif. It was raised from a single piece of copper without the addition of a separate foot. On this example, the stems are enameled with shades of green and white, while stripes of pale blue appear between the stalks, representing the watery environment where ferns grow. Two nature studies of ferns depict the plant in two stages of growth. In one, the fern fronds are closed, and in the second, some fronds are about to open while others have already come to full bloom. Both sketches are signed A.C.G., for Alice C. Gouvy.

The next known vessel in the cylinder-shaped group is a vase in the collection of the Museum of Modern Art, New York, which was raised from a piece of copper, the surface with some type of pepper plant in repoussé. To simulate the plant further, three-dimensional vines were attached to the body, thereby negating its functional purpose. This vase goes beyond a pure utilitarian object, becoming a three-dimensional art form.

I have been able to locate only one piece of Tiffany enamelware with an image other than a plant in the SG series. It is a vase, number 96, and grouped with the above cylindrical examples. It depicts a crane on one side and reeds on the opposite side. Even here, where the principal image is a bird, Tiffany chose to complement it with plant motifs taken from the crane's natural habitat.

Perhaps the most spectacular piece in this group is the vase in the guise of Jack-in-the-pulpits. This piece too was raised from a single piece of copper, the top section cut out after the body was formed. The leaves are

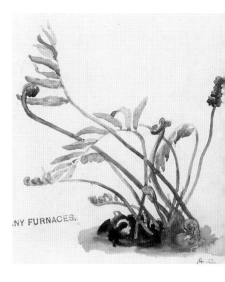

Watercolor drawing of ferns in various stages of growth, and (below) the fronds just before they open. *(Collection of Paula and Howard Ellman).*

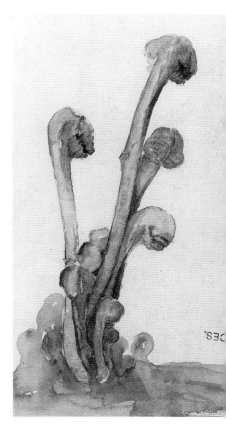

enameled with greens and yellows, typical of the actual plant. Tiffany retained this vase for his personal collection and it was catalogued among the items offered in the Louis Comfort Tiffany Foundation sale of objects from Laurelton Hall in 1946. It was one of two flower vases described as "cylindrical rustic vases, one with reticulated neck molded to simulate jack-in-the-pulpits . . ."[34]

Tiffany made moulds from several of his enamels on metals, and pottery vases and bowls were produced from them. A few examples include the Jack-in-the-pulpit and corn vase[35] and the afore-mentioned tomato bowl, of which   15 the Los Angeles County Museum of Art has both the enameled piece and a pottery version in a bisque finish. A vase decorated with violets, illustrated in Hugh McKean's book, *The "Lost" Treasures of Louis Comfort Tiffany* (Figure 218), is the pottery version of an as yet untraced enamel vase. The outline of the flower heads delineates the lip, as do other examples from this series.

The decoration on the last known example from this group, a vase with maple leaves and seeds in repoussé, is closely based on its nature sketch,   16 signed by Alice Gouvy. In both the sketch and the finished piece, leaves hang from branches, colored in similar tints of greens and blues. On the enameled vase, veins on the leaves and seeds are etched into the surface to give additional detailing.[36]

Tiffany was to return to the cylindrical form in the SG series at a later date. In the interim, he experimented with other forms, starting with rounded shapes. A bowl in the Charles Hosmer Museum of American Art was designed with a hipped outline.[37] Dutchman's pipes were created on the surface by repoussé; the plant bends to follow the contour of the bowl as it rises from the base to the lip. The stem is planted in dirt at the base of the vase, the metal chased to simulate clumps of mud.

The bowl with the Dutchman's pipes is number 123 in the SG series. The next group of objects, small covered boxes, begins with number 161.[38] These resemble pyxis from the Greek archaic period, as well as unguent boxes in which medicinal ointments and salves were stored, examples of which Tiffany collected and used as models for his creations.

Up to this point, all the enameled objects produced in Tiffany's workshop had been open vessels. The box posed additional problems for the craftsman since it had to be made in two steps, the body and the lid, which then had to be fitted together. There are five known small covered boxes in this format. In the case of numbers 161,[39] 187 and 190, decorated with cherries, berries and maple seeds respectively, the motifs are painted onto the surface, as on the earlier enamelware. Within this grouping, however, Tiffany also experimented with champlevé enameling. The only extant examples known, numbers 198 (a piece from Tiffany's loan to the Metropolitan Museum of Art) and 208, are decorated

An unfinished watercolor and pencil sketch signed by A. C. Gouvy for Tiffany's vase with maple seeds and leaves. *(Collection of Paula and Howard Ellman)*.

Three examples of Tiffany's smaller covered boxes. The chrysanthemum design on the box in the middle was champlevé enameled, an unusual technique for Tiffany, who preferred painted enamels, as on the two other examples. *(Center box, Lillian Nassau Ltd.; the other two, collection of Paula and Howard Ellman).*

A watercolor sketch of hawthorn berries. *(Collection of Paula and Howard Ellman).*

with stylized flowers, in contrast to the naturalistic rendering on his other pieces. Perhaps the constraints of working within restricted areas hampered his natural creativity.

The decoration on one covered box is a stylized plant form in which the area between the stems and branches was dug out and filled in with enamel; the stems, branches and knob are gilded. At this stage, gilding was not a new technique on Tiffany's enamelware, since the underside of most of his earlier pieces was finished in this manner. But this was his first attempt at combining these two techniques in order to achieve an unusual palette. The same technique is evident on another covered box on which stylized chrysanthemums are separated from a green background. Both the lid and the body of this box were spun on a lathe, not raised in Tiffany's usual manner; this is a more expeditious method of forming metal.

After exploring the small box format, Tiffany returned one last time to the vase form, re-emphasizing the growth pattern of plants. The first known example from this series is a vase[40] with fuchsia blossoms, buds and leafage in repoussé. The bright yellow colorations, with splashes of olive green in the upper section, contrast with the dark blue and magenta in the lower portion. Tiffany's juxtaposition of a variety of hues was characteristic of his continuing mastery of color. The repoussé decoration protrudes slightly above the lip, with only part of the branch and leaf visible. Morning glories are treated in a similar manner on a vase that Tiffany displayed at the 1902 Turin Exposition.[41]

17

A watercolor sketch of berries signed by L. A. Palmie and dated 12 September 1902. *(Charles Hosmer Morse Museum of American Art, Winter Park, FL).*

The last group in the SG series consists of covered boxes, made on a much larger scale than those discussed above. I know of seven examples, with numbers ranging from 300 to 328. The first few combine two decorative media: glass and enamels on metal. Favrile glass has been blown into the metal mounts in a method similar to that used in Tiffany's blown-out glass lamps, a technique explained by Horace Townsend in his review of the exhibition at the Grafton Galleries, "Lamp bowls . . . are constructed in metal-work of an open reticulated design. In these the glass bowl is placed, and then when hot it is blown outwards, bulging through the open spaces of the metal-work."[42]

The first example in this group of covered boxes is in the Metropolitan Museum of Art; enameled apple tree branches cover the favrile glass base. The leaves are a combination of greens and yellows with splashes of blue, and the apples are composed of various hues of reds over gold foil, giving them a rich, lustrous patina, much like the real fruit. The branches were enameled a muddy grey brown to simulate their natural state; the coloration continues onto the framework of the box. It appears that all the colors were applied at one time, and the piece fired only once.[43] There is only one other extant box executed in a similar manner; it has flowering dogwood branches over a favrile glass body.[44]

The numbering sequence of the other five boxes in this group ranges from 321 to 328. Number 321 is an ovoid jar with a domed cover, with magnolia blossoms and leafage in repoussé, similar to the illustration of lot No. 314 in the Tiffany Foundation sale in 1946.[45] The next four boxes are identical in shape, a circular body with domed cover, the design continuous from the lid to the body. Number 323 is decorated with flowering trumpet vine branches,[46] while number 328 has multi-hued purple and mauve plums in repoussé.[47] Although the next two covered boxes are decorated with grape vines, their conception is quite different. On one, the fruit and leaves are executed in opaque enameling, whereas the other is composed of a combination of iridescent and matte enameling. On the former, the fruit, leaves and vines are set against a mottled blue-and-white background; on the latter, the leaves and fruit are iridized, contrasting with the matte enameled roughened tree trunk that makes up the body of the piece. Vines spread across the bodies of both pieces but in one a thickened branch was designed to function as a handle. Although both boxes were decorated in the identical manner, it appears that Tiffany preferred the latter, for it was part of his display at the Paris Salon in 1906.[48]

As far as we can determine, this is the last group in the SG series on which Tiffany worked. These vessels would date to 1902, the final year the Stourbridge Glass Co. was in operation before being reorganized into Tiffany Furnaces. This occurred sometime in that year but the exact date is unknown.

18

Documents in the Tiffany & Co. archives record an arrangement between the Tiffany Furnaces and the Allied Arts Company, by which the former provided glass to the latter for use in their manufacture of glass windows, as well as acting as agents in the sale of their favrile glassware.[49] This legal document was dated 21 November 1902, which would indicate that by this date Stourbridge Glass Co. had already been taken over by Tiffany Furnaces.

It is not known when Tiffany first began to create those enamel pieces marked with EL. It is likely that this happened shortly after he started making his enamelware. When all the known objects with these stamps are examined, it becomes apparent that most of them were executed on an openly experimental basis; the conception, scale and scope of their coloration and forms are totally different from those pieces executed in the SG series. It would also seem logical that pieces in this series may relate to those in the SG series; certain enameling techniques and colors may have been tested on these vessels and then used on those in the SG series. Perhaps the EL stands for experimental—but why then would a period occasionally appear after each initial? It is to be hoped that documentary evidence may yet come to light which will help sort out these initial designations.

The experimentation on enamelware that Tiffany conducted in the SG series was carried out at a more highly developed level. The objects were formally conceived, and the decoration carefully thought out in conjunction with the shape of the vessel. In the case of many pieces in the EL series, Tiffany was interested in the physical properties of enamel and how it would react when painted onto the surface of metal rather than on the overall shape. Most of these pieces were test items. By heating the enamels at various temperatures, he allowed random effects to control the outcome.[50] He was seeking to produce objects with images unlike anything that he or anyone else had ever conceived. Tiffany cherished this area of his oeuvre, as we can tell by the number of pieces he retained from this series for his personal collection. Although the catalogue of the Tiffany Foundation sale does not give the markings for his enamelware, a rough calculation reveals that out of the 90 pieces he retained, approximately 65 were from the EL series. In 1925, through the Tiffany Foundation, Tiffany offered as a loan to the Metropolitan Museum of Art a selection of glass, enamels, one piece of pottery and a wooden box, "... all representing the highest development of his style from 1897 to 1913."[51] Of the fifteen enamels he presented, nine were EL pieces, a further proof of how highly he valued this series.

21

Unlike groupings in the SG series, in which distinct areas are well defined within a specific numbering code, most enamels marked with EL do not follow structured guidelines. They are loosely categorized, and similar forms are often repeated but not numbered sequentially. Whereas most of the pieces in the

Many of Tiffany's enamels on copper in the EL series are decorated with an impressionistic rendering of plants; this small vase, for instance, depicts some sort of tree. *(Collection of Paula and Howard Ellman)*.

The somewhat later covered box, above right, is unusual for Tiffany in having a black background and being decorated in repoussé with iridized orange salamanders. *(Collection of Jason Ellman)*.

SG series tend to be iridized, this technique is used sparingly in the EL series. However, it is still possible to identify distinct groupings within this series.

The first such group consists of small ovoid vases, their surface enameled with blotches of color. There are three known examples, all in the same shape, numbers 1, 14 and 19.[52] On each piece, the rim is finished with a gold band. On one, the surface has been enameled orange and green; its design is an impressionistic rendering of a tree. Many of the enamels in this classification are decorated with impressionistic and/or expressionistic motifs, designs which are not typical of Tiffany's oeuvre and may represent a glimpse ahead to the modernist art movement.

The next group, an assortment of bowls, vases and covered boxes with numbers from 30 to 130, are related to objects in the SG series, but conceived on a much smaller scale. Although they often follow naturalistic motifs, the images do not always depict recognizable plant forms. A small vase in the Metropolitan's collection, number 39, is decorated with an abstract design of perhaps a spore or some microscopic plant organism. The interior was counter-enameled, which impedes further oxidation of copper and prevents the metal from caving in during heating. An object need not be counter-enameled if the enamel is thinner than the metal. One example of this is decorated with red blotches in a floral design in a thin layer. This particular vase or wide-mouthed bowl was exhibited by Tiffany in the 1904 St. Louis Louisiana Purchase Exposition, illustrated in *The Art of Louis C. Tiffany* and included in his loan to the Metropolitan Museum of Art in 1925.[53] It must have been a piece he was particularly proud of.

Numbers 60 to 113 are small covered boxes and bowls, all with different shapes and decorative treatment. The surface of the first example is in repoussé with salamanders, a rare image on Tiffany's enamelware. The iridized orange reptiles are arranged in a circular pattern on a glossy black background— unusual colors for Tiffany, who preferred gradations of hues rather than pure colors. The covered bowl number 76 is not patterned on conventional forms but is in the shape of an eggplant. The lid has been enameled in iridescent shades of purple and pink with touches of blue, similar to Tiffany's favrile glassware. On the covered bowl number 113, leaves are made up of thickly applied opaque red enamel, outlined by an overlay of silver and gold on a copper ground.

28

Along with this covered box series, Tiffany was also producing bowls, large and small. The smaller versions are decorated in repoussé with fruits and flowers in iridescent enamels which, although not rendered in the shape of the plant depicted, bear similarities to the large bowls in the SG series. Rims were thickened by bending copper over the lip. A bowl with violets, which was part of Tiffany's loan to the Metropolitan Museum of Art, is loosely based on a nature sketch which illustrates two arrangements of flowers, one with several single-stemmed violets arranged in a manner similar to the bowl. There are two additional drawings of violets; one in the Corning Museum, number 231, and one in the Charles Hosmer Morse Museum of American Art, number 232.

24

Tiffany produced several identically shaped spherical bowls with unusual iridescent enameling. One has been inscribed only with his facsimile, another one with his facsimile and an X100 marking where, according to Robert Koch, the "X" means experimental.[54] A third bowl is marked EL 101. The surface of all three was enameled expressionistically with blotches of color in order to achieve unusual colorations. On one piece the green enamel was allowed to flow over the undercoat, which was then peeled back to reveal a charred reddish background similar to hot coals in a fire. Like most of the items in the EL series, these bowls were experiments with the purpose of determining unusual effects in enameling.

Within the EL series, Tiffany produced several desk accessories and trays in which actual plant forms are transposed into enamelware shapes. In a few selected pieces, he did not copy the plant form onto the surface of the vessel but let the actual form dictate the shape of the object. Numbers begin at about 169 and continue up to 210, although not every item in the numerical sequence follows this pattern.

A watercolor sketch used to work out the placement of violets on a bowl now in the Metropolitan Museum of Art. *(Collection of Paula and Howard Ellman)*.

This enamel-on-copper bowl is an example of an enameling technique Tiffany never used elsewhere. Green enamel was peeled back to expose the undercoat. *(Charles Hosmer Morse Museum of American Art, Winter Park, FL)*.

Tiffany's enamel-on-copper inkstand in the guise of a cluster of mushrooms in its natural grassy environment. He retained this object for his own collection. *(The Chrysler Museum, Norfolk, VA. Gift of Walter Chrysler, Jr.).*

The desk tray with milkweed pod motif, number 169,[55] duplicates the actual plant, including its insides in a small lidded compartment. An inkstand is disguised as a cluster of seven mushrooms growing in a clump of grass, imitating their natural habitat. One mushroom cap lifts to accommodate an ink pot, thus converting this three-dimensional sculptural form into a functional object. Iridescent colors of brown, green, rose, yellow, and blue recall Tiffany's favrile glass. Blues and greens with white patches make up the gills on the undersides of the mushroom caps.

After experimenting with the replication of actual plant forms, Tiffany took this idea a step further by depicting a marshy environment on a three-dimensional letter rack, but arranged like a landscape painting with a foreground, middle ground and background. Jack-in-the-pulpit flowers and leaves, growing on the bank and depicted on two partitions, form the background and middle ground, while the pond, alive with reeds and a frog, makes up the foreground. The repoussé flowers and leaves are in low relief in contrast to the high relief of the frog as he pokes his head out of the water. The frog is also captured on a paperweight, where he sits on lily ponds floating in water.[56] In both the inkstand and the letter rack, Tiffany was attempting to cross the boundary between the decorative and fine arts by creating enamel objects which were not only utilitarian but also works of art. These two pieces were retained by Tiffany for his personal collection, and subsequently sold at the Tiffany Foundation sale in 1946.[57]

29

The EL 200 group includes many small pin trays, boxes, and bowls, of which there are examples in the collections of the Charles Hosmer Morse Museum of American Art[58] and the Metropolitan Museum of Art. The covered bowl number 201, produced during the time Tiffany was creating his 28 sculptural desk items, is rendered in the guise of a ripening raspberry. The texture of the bowl, roughened to simulate the exterior of the berry, is enameled in shades from orange to purple to represent the gradual ripening process. Leaves and berries decorate the surface.

Tiffany designed enamels, perhaps as many as 100, that did not fall within either the SG or EL designations. Some of them he created for his own collection, never intending to offer them for sale. They were either included in the 1925 loan to the Metropolitan or kept in his collection at Laurelton Hall.

A tray in the shape of a gourd is not marked but has been identified as Tiffany's through an illustration in the Tiffany Foundation sale.[59] A liqueur set in the Japanese taste, produced by Tiffany & Co. in 1878, included a tray in the shape of a gourd,[60] and this may have been the inspiration for Tiffany's enamel gourd tray, since both the shape and decoration, including a stem protruding from the rim, are similar. Instead of coating the surface with sentoku, a copper patination, Tiffany enameled it a mottled green and yellow, more in keeping with the natural colors of gourds.

Other objects that Tiffany retained for his private collection were marked "A-COLL", a mark which also appears on his favrile glass as well as on selected pieces of enamelware. According to the 1919 inventory of Laurelton Hall, there were "unusual examples of Favrile glass of brilliant coloring and unique forms, also enameled pottery . . . collection numbers about 400 objects."[61] Tiffany selected unique examples from his workshop which represented a certain style or technique.

I know of only four Tiffany enamels on metal that bear this mark, preceded by a three-digit number, 153, 154, 157 and 162. These items may have been originally created during the course of Tiffany's normal enamelware production, but after they were completed, he decided to keep them for himself, marking them in this special way at a later date. Two of the items (153 and 157) were included in the loan to the Metropolitan Museum of Art. The first, a covered bowl, was champlevé enameled, then patinated, giving the appearance of a silver and copper surface which resembles Japanese lacquer ware. This piece also has a "Tiffany Studios" paper label attached to the underside. The second item is a vase in an Oriental double gourd shape, a common form in Tiffany's favrile glassware. He retained this vase because of the unique expressionistic enamel which was allowed to "run" over the gold background, achieved through the use of transparent glazes.

A box in the collection of the Virginia Museum of Fine Arts is   23
numbered 154. Three cicadas with outstretched wings encircle an irregularly
shaped lid. On the top of the lid are three cicadas with their wings folded, their
bodies forming the handle. An article in *The Craftsman* from 1904, which
illustrates a study of a locust with its wings open and closed, may have given
Tiffany the idea for this use of the motif.[62] The mark on this box indicates that it
was part of Tiffany's private collection, a fact confirmed by a photograph in
Gertrude Speenburgh's *The Arts of the Tiffanys*, which shows a cabinet with
"Tiffany crafts housed at Laurelton Hall."[63]

The fourth item, a large bowl decorated with Dutchman's pipes
in repoussé[64] was marked SG 123 along with "162 A-COLL". A fifth item, a pin
cushion in the collection of the Chrysler Museum of Art, is incised with a three-   26
digit number, 531, but lacks the "A-COLL" designation, although it was one of
the items in Tiffany's collection.[65] As far as we can tell, this is the only piece
marked in this manner. Orange and yellow nasturtiums, intermingled with
leaves, decorate the perimeter while green velvet, rather worn, simulates grass
and protrudes above the surface.

Several pieces of Tiffany's enamelware are marked with a four-
digit number preceded by an "S." Since there are only a handful of such objects
available, it may be that Tiffany designed them for himself, or to fulfil special
commissions. The Tiffany & Co. archives contains many drawings marked
"S.O." for items sold as commissioned. Perhaps "S" was Louis Tiffany's way of
identifying those earmarked for an exhibition, a special client, or himself.

An urn-shaped covered jar, number S 1161, is the first in this
series. Although it bears a Tiffany number, it was not signed by him, indicating
that it was most likely part of his own collection. It was exhibited in Tiffany's
display at the 1900 Exposition Universelle in Paris, and was also illustrated in
several journals, including *Brush and Pencil*, *Deutsche Kunst und Dekoration*,
and a review of the exhibition by Roger Marx, *La Décoration et Les Industries
d'Art à L'Exposition Universelle de 1900*.[66] Indian pipes were enameled onto the
surface so thickly that the decoration appears at first glance to be repoussé in low
relief. As we have seen, most of Tiffany's enamels on metal were either enameled
on repoussé bodies or, in a few cases, champlevé enameled. This piece achieves a
similar raised effect simply by enameling without disturbing the metal.

Although an urn-shaped covered jar is a conventional form by
today's standards, especially when compared to pieces directly inspired by plant
forms, at the time it was exhibited Gardner Teall described it as "An Exquisite
Design" in his article in *Brush and Pencil*.[67]

A three-handled vase, numbered S 1285 and impressed with   22
"Tiffany Studios New York" as well as a Tiffany Glass & Decorating Co. logo,

This urn-shaped enamel-on-copper covered jar, shown at the 1900 Exposition Universelle in Paris, was thickly enameled to give the effect of repoussé. The lower section is enameled in light shades of green. *(Private collection)*.

was made about 1900, the year the firm's name was changed to Tiffany Studios. Although there is no documentary proof that this vase was exhibited in the Paris Exposition or at any other international world's fair, Tiffany did illustrate it in *The Art of Louis Comfort Tiffany* and retained it for his collection.[68] Two- and three-handled vessels are normally called "loving cups", a term used for large drinking vessels that are circulated among guests at banquets or other festive gatherings. Multiple side handles enhanced the convenience in handing the cup from person to person. Although this vessel has been called a vase due to the addition of a liner, the caption in *The Art of Louis Comfort Tiffany* describes it as a cup. The grape motif on the repoussé surface and repeated in the gilt vine-shaped handles is correlated with the actual function of the piece—drinking wine.

Tiffany created several pieces of enamelware which do not bear any letter designations, but are marked with a four-digit number in the 9,000 sequence, followed by another number. The first number denoted a specific form, the additional number indicated a different decorative motif. There may have been up to ten versions of the same item. A covered box with an octopus-like design on the lid is marked 9041/10. An identically shaped box, offered in

10

Sotheby's "Important Art Nouveau and Art Deco" sale on 19 November 1983 (lot No. 678), was enameled with a frog seated on a lily pad and marked 9041/3. A vase in Sotheby's "Important Tiffany and Other Art Nouveau" sale on 24 March 1984 (lot No. 174) is inscribed *Louis C. Tiffany/Tiffany Studios/New York/9150/ 9*. This shape, designated by 9150, is enameled with poppies; other versions were probably decorated with different flowers. A few Tiffany enamels are marked "Tiffany Studios." A covered box, number 9151/1, is part of the Tiffany loan to the Metropolitan Museum of Art. The background is hammered, then opaque enameled to give a matte surface. A grasshopper and some type of red beans, resembling coffee beans, decorate the lid in low relief, achieved by a thick layer of enamel rather than by the repoussé process. An identical item, offered at Sotheby's "20th Century Decorative Arts" sale, 8 and 9 June 1988 (lot No. 461), had a lid decorated with two grasshoppers. The catalogue listing records the number as 9150/10; this may be a misreading or the piece was mismarked, because the number should coincide with the box in the Metropolitan's collection and read 9151/10.

A watercolor sketch by Alice Gouvy of a dandelion plant before the flowers have turned to seed-balls. The dandelion seed-ball, with its soft, feathery head and subtle colorations, was a source of inspiration for Tiffany, and can be seen in a dandelion lamp and jewelry that he showed at the 1904 St. Louis exhibition. *(The Corning Museum of Glass)*.

Within this 9,000 series, Tiffany created a stamp box marked *Tiffany Studios/New York/9396*. It is in the shape of a rhinoceros beetle and relates to the three-dimensional desk items made in the EL series, such as the mushroom inkstand. It was illustrated in *The Craftsman*, May 1902, which enables us to date it between 1900, the date when the name Tiffany Glass & Decorating Company was changed to Tiffany Studios, and early 1902.[69]

There are a few known items stamped with a four-digit 8,000 number. One, a box in the Charles Hosmer Morse Museum marked 8589, has matte enameling and the lid is decorated with bubbles. Plaques also fall within this series, such as an example, numbered 8319, in a private collection which is decorated in repoussé with leaves and some type of pods. Another known plaque is the only extant piece of Tiffany's enamelware marked with a five-digit number, 89451. Executed in iridescent enameling, a composition of seaweed, oyster and mussel shells forms an interesting play of colors and shapes.

At the outset of Tiffany's exploration into enameling on metals, he created several lamps either with enameled bases or embellished with enameled decorative motifs. One such lamp with a base enameled with dandelions was exhibited as part of S. Bing's Art Nouveau exhibition at the 1900 Exposition Universelle in Paris and in Tiffany's display at the 1901 Buffalo Pan-American Exposition, when it was illustrated in *Keramic Studio*.[70] The stems and leaves make up the shaft of the body, crowned by dandelion puffs from which spring the blown glass shade. Two drawings of dandelions show different views of the plant: number 95 depicts the entire plant with leaves and yellow flowers, whereas number 92 shows two stages in the life of the flower after it has lost its

Elektrische Lampen und Kerzenhalter der *Tiffany Glass & Decorating Co.,* *New York.* (Nach Originalaufnahmen.)

Taf. 57.

Verlag von Jul. Hoffmann, Stuttgart.

bloom. (An additional pink flower unrelated to dandelions has been sketched in the right-hand corner.) Two sketches show the flower before it is about to open into a puff ball and after the puffs have been dispersed. Tiffany made a second version of this lamp,[71] impressed with S 1340 and stamped *Tiffany Glass & Decorating Company*, the parent organization of Stourbridge Glass Co. This lamp must have been made prior to 1900, since after 2 April 1900 the name Tiffany Glass & Decorating Company was no longer used.

The majestic and colorful peacock had become a popular motif with designers on both sides of the Atlantic throughout the Art Nouveau period. Its brilliant feathers with ever-changing iridescent colors were bound to be an irresistible lure to Louis Tiffany, the master colorist, and indeed he incorporated the motif in all media of his oeuvre. At the 1901 Pan-American exhibition, in addition to the dandelion lamp, he showed a peacock lamp. In this piece, Tiffany combined his favorite media, favrile glass and enameling, to create a functional object. It was illustrated in *The Jewelers' Review* and described as "the famous peacock lamp, with favrile glass stem three feet high, peacock feather decorations surmounted by three peacock heads supporting a favrile glass globe with necklace

This page from *Der Moderne Stil*, v. 3, pl. 57, illustrates some of Tiffany's lamps, including the dandelion model with an enameled base and blown glass shade, and the first of several versions of his famous "peacock" lamp. Both were shown at the 1901 Pan-American Exposition in Buffalo. *(Collection of Gladys and Robert Koch)*.

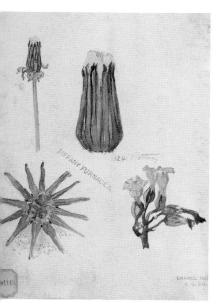

Several sketches were often drawn for particular plants, especially those that were Tiffany's favorites. In this drawing, two sketches of a dandelion show 1) the flower after it has closed with the puffs just visible, and 2) the inside of the flower after the puffs have blown away. *(Charles Hosmer Morse Museum of American Art, Winter Park, FL).*

or group of scarab shaped drops."[72] This lamp epitomizes Gardner Teall's assessment that Tiffany "had probably done the most of any one practically toward forwarding a feeling for the beautiful as applied to our necessities."[73]

Three enameled peacock heads encircle the upper section of the favrile glass body, appearing to support the favrile glass globe. The flaring foot has been enameled and contains "eyes" from the feather while a necklace of enameled scarabs hangs just below the globe. Tiffany made several versions of this lamp. One has an orange-toned favrile glass body and matching globe, with an enameled double-strand necklace of scarabs.[74] He designed another for Charles Gould which, like the one exhibited in the Pan-American Exposition, features three peacock heads enameled in blue tones to correspond with the same colorings in the favrile glass body. Instead of decorating the neck of the lamp with scarabs, the necklace has been suspended from the neck of each peacock, interconnected with the next peacock to form a breastplate.[75] It is also interesting that the beetle necklaces Tiffany designed, beginning in 1909, are exactly the same as those on these lamps.

30

Tiffany's venture into enameling has to be viewed as an intense and successful phase of his artistic life. Within two years of launching this new endeavor, he exhibited selected pieces at major international exhibitions and received many favorable reviews. At the 1900 Paris Exposition Universelle a reviewer commented, "Another entirely new and recent discovery is that of the enameling on copper, the enamel being iridescent."[76] On the occasion of the Pan-American Exposition, it was written that "There is an interesting collection of the Tiffany iridescent enamels on metal, in the form of small boxes and vases. We believe this is the first time the iridescent enamels have been used upon metals."[77] Tiffany also showed selections of these items in the "First Annual Exhibition of Original Designs for Decorations and Examples of Art Crafts having Distinct Artistic Merit" held at the Art Institute of Chicago (16 December 1902 to 7 January 1903), the Esposizione d'Arte Decorativa Moderna in Turin in 1902, the 1904 St. Louis Louisiana Purchase Exposition, and the 1906 Paris Salon.[78]

In 1907, Tiffany was ready to move on to the next phase of his association with Tiffany & Co. First his father and then Charles Cook had died, giving way to a new management in which he played a prominent role, thus offering him an uninhibited opportunity to exert the kind of artistic leadership he had been preparing for. That year, he closed his jewelry and enamelware departments at Tiffany Furnaces and transferred his staff to Tiffany & Co., where he continued his creative efforts in this field.

3

Louis Comfort Tiffany's Artistic Jewelry

It is a well established fact that Louis Comfort Tiffany waited until after his father's death in 1902 to begin creating jewelry. It was, however, a combination of personal and corporate circumstances that influenced not only the timing, but also the intensity of his foray into this new venture.

Through skillful management, Charles Lewis Tiffany had elevated Tiffany & Co. to the status of acknowledged arbiter of taste in America during the last half of the 19th century. His shop offered "high style" decorative arts gathered from all parts of the world, as well as Tiffany's own jewelry and silver, which received wide recognition at all the international exhibitions. He died on 17 February 1902, at the age of 90. He had been the patriarch of his family and the active head of Tiffany & Co., which he continued to serve until the end as president of the Board of Directors.

Within a month of Charles Tiffany's death, a special meeting of the Board of Trustees was called on 14 March 1902, to elect new officers. Louis Comfort Tiffany nominated Charles T. Cook, who had been vice-president of the company since 1888, for the presidency, and John C. Moore, son of Edward C. Moore, for vice-president. It was recommended that the by-laws of the company be amended to include the additional office of second vice-president among the roster of officers.[1]

This recommendation, which was to have an important impact on Louis Tiffany's relationship with Tiffany & Co., was approved at an ad hoc meeting of the Board on 22 March. G. B. Berchmans's nomination of Louis Comfort Tiffany to fill this new position was seconded by John C. Moore.[2] From this date until his death in 1933, Tiffany remained a member of Tiffany & Co.'s Board of Directors.

Within a short time after he was elected second vice-president, Louis Tiffany started to share the art direction responsibilities of the company with Paulding Farnham, who had been the Art Director for several years. Although it is not known precisely what all his new responsibilities entailed, one of them was to confer with the architect Stanford White on the new Tiffany & Co.

building that was erected in 1905 at the corner of 37th Street and Fifth Avenue, as well as renovations to the premises in the Avenue de l'Opéra in Paris.[3] Since Tiffany had been involved with many interior decorating commissions, he appears to have been the logical choice to negotiate these matters.

He was also given the responsibility of correcting new designs (it is not clear whether this task was assigned to him or whether he simply assumed it). In one instance, he edited a preliminary sketch for the "Atlas" souvenir spoon, designed by Paulding Farnham, indicating that two putti-type figures should be omitted from the top of the handle. His instructions, "leave figures off . . . this change *ordered* by Mr. L. C. Tiffany May 17/07,"[4] infer that Tiffany felt he could edit even the work of Paulding Farnham, a man who had previously received numerous medals as Tiffany & Co.'s chief designer. In another instance, according to Farnham's son John Farnham, a dispute arose over the nudity of the figure on the Renaissance flatware pattern. Tiffany felt the figure was too revealing; Farnham felt otherwise. Tiffany's opinion obviously prevailed since the actual figure is substantially draped, leaving only her breasts bare.[5]

Thus armed with official corporate authority, and with his father's shadow no longer extending over his every move, Louis Tiffany could now consider undertaking jewelry, a field he had hitherto regarded as off limits.

The jewelry Tiffany & Co. exhibited at international exhibitions from 1889 through 1902 had all been designed under the direction of Farnham. This also held true for silverware at the 1900 Exposition Universelle in Paris and the 1901 Pan-American Exposition in Buffalo. However, after Louis Tiffany took an active role in the art direction of Tiffany & Co., Farnham's jewelry was no longer showcased at these world fairs. In the case of the 1904 Louisiana Purchase Exposition in St. Louis, Farnham contributed an elaborate Florentine-inspired silver service and a single piece of jewelry, a Renaissance style necklace,[6] whereas Tiffany exhibited 27 pieces of *his* jewelry. This is a clear indication that by 1904 Farnham's reign was on the descent.

Tiffany began experimenting with jewelry design in 1902 at Tiffany Furnaces, with the explicit objective of exhibiting pieces as part of Tiffany & Co.'s display at the St. Louis Exposition. He was aware that this venue would give international exposure to what he hoped would be a significant contribution to not only American, but also European jewelry design. What better way for him to make his mark in this new venture than through an appearance at an international fair? After all, since he had succeeded in every area of the decorative arts that he had pursued, there was no reason why he should doubt his ability to achieve similar results with his jewelry creations. He certainly had the background and design expertise to accomplish his aims, as well as capable assistants at Tiffany Furnaces to help realize his creations.

At first, however, Louis Tiffany was skeptical about the final results, and made his preparations in a secretive manner. According to Gertrude Speenburgh, he worked "for two years before anyone was allowed to know that Louis C. Tiffany was experimenting with hand-wrought jewelry,"[7] which he would present for public view at the St. Louis Exposition. The work he showed received favorable reviews that surpassed his most optimistic hopes.

When the department first opened at Tiffany Furnaces, located in a small workshop at the 23rd Street studio, Julia Munson, who had shown promise in Tiffany's enamelware department, was put in charge. She was 27 at the time and, after working for four years under the direction of Patricia Gay and Dr. Parker McIlhinney, she must have shown sufficient aptitude to handle her new responsibilities. It was she, according to Speenburgh, who purchased the gemstones and supplies that were not acquired at Tiffany & Co.; "in case results should be unsatisfactory, or not worthy of their high standards, the public could not attribute the failure to a Tiffany project."[8]

At the beginning, Munson was supported by another young woman. Within a short time, two "gifted Italians," an Irishman, and a Scotsman were added to the staff.[9] This small international band of employees produced almost 400 pieces of jewelry from 1902 to 1907, when the department was absorbed into Tiffany & Co. Himilce Novas quotes Julia Munson Sherman (her married name) as estimating that "Only a few hundred [pieces] were made."[10] This figure can be substantiated by a numbering code on the jewelry illustrated in a photographic scrapbook in the Tiffany & Co. archives collection. Every jewel illustrated has been given a number prefixed by an initial; "J" indicates a piece designed while Julia Munson was in charge of the department. Like Tiffany's earlier enamels on copper, these jewels are arranged consecutively by number. If we compare the known pieces of his jewelry produced before 1907 to those in this scrapbook, the highest number is below 400, thus confirming Munson's approximation.

All the jewelry Louis Tiffany made during this period is stamped "Louis C. Tiffany" in facsimile, along with "Artist." In a few cases, "Artist" has been omitted. I have seen just one exception to this rule, a necklace marked only "LCT" on the clasp. I believe this was one of Tiffany's first attempts at jewelry design, perhaps even predating the formation of his department. It is made up of graduated favrile glass balls alternating with bronze beads, strung on a bronze chain. The simplicity of the design belies the difficulty in making such a necklace. Appropriately sized glass balls must be carefully assembled, each drilled with a hole to accommodate the chain, in the same way that natural pearls are strung on similarly styled necklaces. (Tiffany & Co. was retailing such pearl necklaces at a price far greater than this one with favrile glass balls.)

32

Although no day books or ledgers survive that would provide information about the jewelry Tiffany designed prior to 1907, his exhibit at the St. Louis Exposition offers valuable evidence. In addition to his 27 pieces of jewelry, he provided five enamels on copper, all featured in the "Tiffany Room" of Gallery 28 in the Fine Arts Building, where he shared space with Tiffany & Co.'s display of gold and silver holloware, and the one necklace designed by Paulding Farnham. He also showed pottery and favrile glass in an adjoining gallery.

Louis Tiffany's exhibit attracted much attention and was widely publicized. Reviews appeared in *The Craftsman, The Jewelers' Circular-Weekly, Vogue, The Boston Budget, Washington Life, Town and Country*. In 1906 a few pieces were discussed in an article in *The International Studio*. Most of the information in these publications is repetitive, each giving more or less identical information, an indication that Tiffany or his publicity department may have distributed pre-written releases. Pre-selected objects were described in detail, the reviewers copying the text almost verbatim.

For the most part, the jewelry Tiffany designed for this exposition was based on flowers of "such species as are commonly met in the fields or woods, or yet along country roads: among them being the clover, the wild carrot, the bitter-sweet, the blackberry, the mountain ash, and the spirea,"[11] a theme that is not surprising in view of Tiffany's prior reliance on nature for inspiration. He also contributed two pieces based on Etruscan prototypes.

With the exception of one necklace, the whereabouts of these pieces is unknown. The only evidence of their appearance is black-and-white illustrations in contemporary journals, as well as photographs in two scrapbooks in the Tiffany & Co. archives. Unfortunately, these photographic records are incapable of showing the subtle color arrangements of gemstones and enameling, or the delicate filigree work used as accents on many pieces.

Tiffany combined colored gemstones with enameling on various metals. Of the 27 items exhibited, 14 were made of silver, five of a combination of silver and gold, three of copper, two of gold, and one of platinum and iridium. There are no specific descriptions available for the remaining two pieces. He used such gemstones as carnelians, coral, demantoid garnets, garnets, onyx, topazes, and opals (including the Mexican variety) and opals in matrix. Diamonds were used to accent several pieces that combined both enameling and the above gemstones. On two pieces, a clover blossom tiara and a cranberry sprig brooch, diamonds are the only stones highlighting the enamel. Of the remaining 25 pieces, seven were embellished only with enameling, three with gemstones, and fifteen with both enameling and gemstones.

According to a Tiffany & Co. privately printed pamphlet, Tiffany exhibited three brooches of "lustre enameled copper," one with purple berries, one with grapes, and the third with wire appliqué and set with an opal.[12] The appearance of these three items in the exhibition would indicate that Tiffany had expanded his enamels on copper to include jewelry. I know of only two extant examples of such jewelry, a belt clasp in a private collection, marked "L.C.T. EL260", that was converted into a brooch, and a buckle that is marked simply "L.C.T." The former example was made in the enamelware division of Tiffany Furnaces towards the end of the EL series, while the latter, like the favrile glass necklace mentioned earlier, may have been one of the first examples made in the new department.

33

Tiffany contributed three ornaments based on the wild carrot blossom, better known as Queen Anne's lace, each enameled on silver. One of these was set with demantoid garnets, opals, garnets, and diamonds, while the other two were set with demantoid garnets, red garnets and diamonds. Tiffany was familiar with the Queen Anne's lace motif which he had used earlier in chandeliers for the Havemeyers' music room. The images for these ornaments may have been based on photographs taken by Tiffany, which are now in the Charles Hosmer Morse Museum of American Art.[13] In one photograph, two flower heads are arranged so that their blossoms are viewable from a front angle and not depicted at the end of the stem in umbrella fashion; two of Tiffany's ornaments are also depicted in this manner. An article in *The Craftsman* describes the coiffure ornament as "realistically treated and shown at the height of its bloom. In the center of each section of the flower, fine opals are massed for the production of color-play and each petal is worked out individually in minute detail; while the center of the entire blossom is set with garnets and diamonds, which emphasize the sectional divisions, and serve to increase the fire of the opals."[14] The article illustrates the two other ornaments, which are not described

For the 1904 St. Louis exhibition, Tiffany created a number of ornaments based on wildflowers. The two coiffure ornaments, below left, show wild carrot blossoms (Queen Anne's lace) and are made of silver, enameled and set with demantoid garnets, garnets and diamonds. The two other ornaments depict white enameled flowers, gold stamens, and green translucent enameled leaves. *(Reproduced from* The Craftsman *v. VII (November 1904), 176).*

in the text. A contrast was provided by a silver nanny-berry ornament whose only decoration was enameling: white flowers, filigree green leaves, and berry-like black fruit.

A piece of special interest was a tiara made up of a cluster of clover blossoms and leaves. The blossoms were "of hammered gold, overlaid with yellow enamel, while the leaves and stems, of repoussé and filigree silver, are enameled in green. The effect of the piece is much increased by means of a shower of dew-drops simulated in diamonds which, scattered over the leaves and flowers of the cluster, suggest it has been gathered in the morning."[15] By depicting the plant in its natural environment, with dew on its blossoms and leaves, Tiffany was striving in this piece for more than just a representation of the flower.

Realism was also the theme of three coiffure pieces; one in the shape of a dandelion seed-ball, and the others, sprays of either spirea or blackberry branches. Instead of showing the flower in full bloom, in its most perfect state, Tiffany chose to capture a moment during the growth cycle of the plant. This was a familiar concept to Tiffany, who had used more or less the same theme on many pieces of his enamelware. He would also have been aware of a flower Paulding Farnham exhibited in the 1901 Buffalo Pan-American Exposition, a rare species of carnation, the "Lawson Pink", in which petals are shown in various stages of growth. Tiffany's spirea spray follows Farnham's example, rendered naturalisti-

Tiffany showed this dandelion seed-ball coiffure ornament at the St. Louis exhibition; it is made up of enamel and filigree leaves and buds, tied together by a string. *(Reproduced from* Town and Country, *v. 59 (October 29, 1904), 16).*

A page in *Vogue* devoted to Tiffany's work shown at the 1904 St. Louis exhibition. Vignettes of jewelry are placed amid a grape arbor, a fitting design in view of Tiffany's widespread use of the grape and wine motif. Illustrated from left to right: the spirea spray, the dragonfly hair ornament above a grape-motif necklace (the original version of the necklace in Ill. 36), the blackberry spray above a pendant necklace based on bittersweet, and two brooches with berries. *(Reproduced from* Vogue, *v. XXIV (December 1, 1904), 702).*

ST. LOUIS EXPOSITION JEWELRY

cally with flowers in full bloom and a cluster of buds partially opened. The flowers are enameled white on stamens of gold wire ending in a small gold ball.

In the case of the blackberry spray, the leaves are made of filigree silver filled with translucent enamel.

The berries are of carnelians and garnets, each separately carved, and all so arranged in various shades of color that the berries are shown in different stages of ripening, from the faintest tint of pink to the darkest hue of the fully matured fruit. Each pistil of the berry is a separately carved stone, all so joined and fastened on the stem that the metal used is entirely hidden, making the berry in its form, color, and texture a perfect simulation of nature.[16]

For the dandelion seed-ball, Tiffany reproduced the puff just before it is scattered by the wind. Tiny white opals set on the ends of silver wire make up the seed-ball, suggesting "the dispersal of the seeds by the slightest touch."[17] To add to the realism, Tiffany displayed the dandelion seed-ball ornament along with three buds and several enameled dandelion leaves, tied together by a string.

On each of the above examples, Tiffany captured a moment in the life of the plant, either as it was growing to maturity or disseminating its seeds, much in the manner of stop-action photography. According to Hugh McKean, Tiffany was an avid photographer, who took snapshots of ordinary people going about their everyday lives, and intentionally cropped many images to emphasize features of the human face or parts of buildings. McKean cites an article in *The International Studio* which discusses Tiffany's early involvement with photography when "he shared with Edward Muybridge the honor of being the first to take instantaneous photographs of birds and animals in motion."[18] With a background of analyzing life and nature through the camera lens, Tiffany understood the minute intricacies of a natural phenomenon such as the opening of a flower, and could depict them quite naturally in his jewelry creations.

Tiffany continued to experiment not only with the design of pieces of jewelry but also with new metals, such as platinum, which at the time was generally considered a difficult metal to work. He contributed two platinum ornaments to his display at the St. Louis Exposition; one in the guise of a bunch of sage-seed vessels and the other a dragonfly. On the former, the vessels were made out of platinum (described by a reviewer in *The Jewelers' Circular-Weekly* as "a special metal") and filled with translucent enamel to simulate the actual plant.[19] Although jewelry with platinum-mounted gemstones backed with gold had been popular since the 1890s, solid platinum was not widely used until about 1910, which explains why the writer reported it as he did.

31. One of Tiffany's early experiments with geometric configurations beginning in 1907, this necklace combines Mexican fire opals, green enameling and pearls against a gold ground. *(Virginia Museum of Fine Arts, Gift of Sydney and Frances Lewis)*.

32. This necklace of graduated favrile glass beads is one of Tiffany's first jewelry designs. *(Collection of Paula and Howard Ellman)*.

33. A buckle decorated with enameled pea pods. (*Collection of Lillian Nassau*).

34, 35. A gold brooch with a central rosette consisting of six opals and one demantoid garnet set into chrysoprase; date 1907, signed "Louis C. Tiffany Artist," as can be seen on the edge. *(Collection of Paula and Howard Ellman)*.

36. This enlarged version of a gold necklace of opals and green enamel which was originally shown by Tiffany at the 1904 St. Louis fair was owned by Tiffany's nurse-companion, Sarah Hanley. *(Metropolitan Museum of Art, Gift of Sarah E. Hanley, 1946)*.

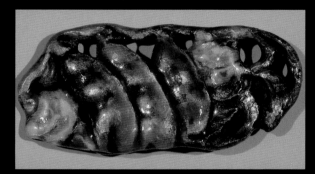

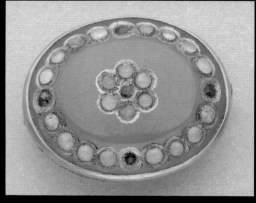

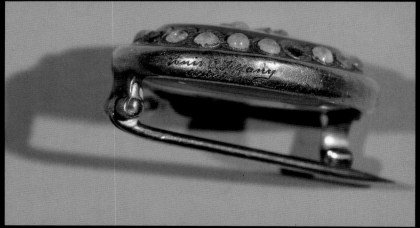

38. A gold bib necklace, incorporating seed pearls and baroque pearl drops, which was made in 1906, a year before Louis Comfort Tiffany's jewelry division became part of Tiffany & Co.

37. A pendant based on the medusa jellyfish that was shown at St. Louis in 1904 and at the Paris Salon of 1906. The body is made up of opals surrounded by sapphires with demantoid garnets and rubies studded along the tentacles. It was owned by Henry Walters of Baltimore, but its present whereabouts are unknown.

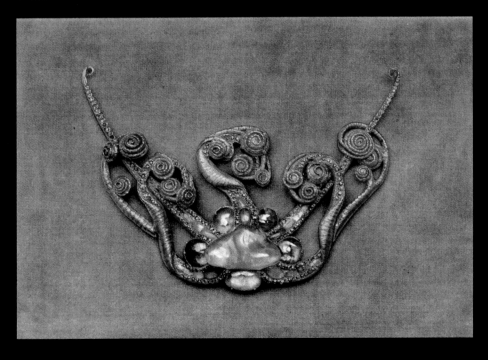

39, 40. An enameled "peacock" necklace made in about 1905. The medallion on the obverse is decorated with a mosaic of peacocks in opals; other stones include amethysts, sapphires, demantoid garnets, rubies and emeralds. After completing the necklace, Tiffany felt that the reverse was too bare and designed enameled plaques for the medallion and lappets decorated with flamingoes. *(Charles Hosmer Morse Museum of American Art, Winter Park, FL).*

41. The motif of two peacocks
facing each other was first used in
this mosaic for the Havemeyer
house, *c.* 1891, and then again in
the chapel Tiffany designed for
the 1893 Chicago exhibition.
*(University of Michigan School of
Art and College of Architecture
and Urban Planning, on
extended loan to the University
of Michigan Museum of Art).*

The same reviewer also described the dragonfly's wings as made out of a special metal; this is explained in an article in *The International Studio* as "a special alloy of iridium and platinum."[20] In order to duplicate the gossamer spider-web effect of the wings, Tiffany chose this alloy since it had the strength to be woven into delicate filaments, simulating the actual insect's wings. This effect could not be achieved with traditional jewelry metals such as gold and silver. Opals and opalines formed the head and body of the dragonfly, while the back was studded with demantoid garnets. Tiffany chose this dragonfly hair ornament for his display at the 1906 Paris Salon[21] and a few years later, he transposed the motif into a brooch, almost duplicating its form and materials.

36 Stones with unusual colorations appealed to Tiffany, especially those with a mottled appearance, such as opals. On one of the necklaces he showed in St. Louis, opalines simulate grapes arranged in clusters, the central portion set with an opal in matrix surrounded by enameled grape leaves. This is the only surviving piece of jewelry from the Exposition and is now in the collection of the Metropolitan Museum of Art. In its original state when exhibited in St. Louis and illustrated in *Vogue*, four clusters were arranged on a simple twisted gold wire. At some point, three additional clusters were added, two attached to the central section and one to the clasp, while the wire was replaced by solid links.

In St. Louis, Tiffany also exhibited four brooches with opals; one with purple berries set into enameled copper, two with flowers in silver and enamel, and the last a yellow flower, set with two Mexican opals. Other brooches included a cluster of mountain ash berries, enameled on silver and set with coral, and a cranberry sprig in enameled gold with silver enameled leaves, sprinkled with diamonds. On each of these brooches, stones are partially concealed within their enameled mountings in the natural colorations of leaves, flowers and berries.

The motif on a pendant necklace (called a girdle in the literature) is based on the Solanum Ducamara, or bitter-sweet, a climbing plant of the deadly nightshade family. Tiffany matched the berries' unique scarlet colors precisely with delicately enameled repoussé silver and carved Mexican opals and carnelians; the variety of materials and stones provides a contrast in colors as well as textures. The berries are arranged in bunches which diminish in size from the center cluster to the clasp ends, their gold stems woven into a vine-like structure forming the band. This piece impressed many critics; the article in *The Craftsman* compared it to the work of René Lalique. "Its boldness counterfeits the hand of Lalique himself; while its delicacy and availability to use places it beyond many of the productions of that master, which are museum objects rather than articles fitted for personal adornment and use. It is a masterpiece of

American craftsmanship and, at the same time, an artistic creation of great value."[22]

Besides the dragonfly ornament, Tiffany showed another piece based on a living creature, a pendant in the shape of a medusa, that is, a jellyfish, not to be confused with one of the terrible Gorgon sisters of Greek mythology. The catalogue entry from the Tiffany & Co. brochure of the exposition states that the piece was made of gold, enameled, and set with carved opals and other precious stones which, according to Charles DeKay, who describes it as a brooch, are sapphires and rubies.[23] The main body of the creature is an opal in matrix that appears to be surrounded by cabochon sapphires. Rubies adorn the tentacles that rise up from the body and form small "eyes" from which ribbons would be attached while demantoid garnets, as specified in a photograph album in the Tiffany & Co. archives, are set along other tentacles. The gold has been carefully worked in repoussé to reproduce the scaly body of the fish.

Tiffany exhibited the medusa pendant in the 1906 Paris Salon along with the dragonfly hair ornament, an enameled brooch set with what appears to be an opal, and a fringe necklace with amethysts and jade.[24] Henry Walters bought the medusa pendant, although it is not known when. It was illustrated in *The Art of Louis Comfort Tiffany* in 1914, and was subsequently sold in the Parke-Bernet sale of Mrs. Henry Walters's estate on 2 December 1943, where it was catalogued as "Opal, Olivine and Gold Pendant . . . In the form of Medusa, some stones missing; back signed Louis C. Tiffany, Artist."[25] Its current whereabouts are unknown.

As mentioned earlier, the Tiffany exhibit at St. Louis included two enameled necklaces based on Etruscan jewelry, one in gold and the other in silver. The silver necklace, based on Etruscan strap necklaces, was set with

Tiffany showed two necklaces at the St. Louis exhibition based on Etruscan models. On this silver necklace, the collar was made up of 400 enameled cup forms, from which five rows of rosettes were suspended. Green and blue enameling accentuated sapphires and demantoid garnets. *(Reproduced in* The Craftsman, *v. VII (November 1904), 178).*

sapphires and demantoid garnets, in the form of a collar with five rows of rosettes gradually diminishing in size. It was reviewed in *The Jewelers' Circular-Weekly* and *The Boston Budget*, both describing it in the identical words:

> The collar is an arrangement of four rows of small enameled silver cup forms, about four hundred in all, the rows ending in two clasp bosses of a conventionalized flower form. Part of the pendant rows are of conventionalized flower design with a green Garnet in the centre of each setting, and the other rows are clusters of enameled silver cup forms, linked together with set sapphires. From the pendant bands hang pear-shaped Sapphires. The enameling is translucent in quality and shaded in green and blue to blend with the gems.[26]

It was greatly admired at the Exposition and was described as "beautiful enough to have been exhumed from a tomb of Chiusi or Volterra."[27]

The numbers assigned to the St. Louis pieces begin somewhere around 100, prefixed of course by the letter "J" for Julia Munson, who directed their manufacture. The blackberry spray is J101; the necklace with grape clusters and ovals now in the Metropolitan Museum of Art is J110; the dragonfly hair ornament J117; the medusa pendant J123; and the spirea spray J149. There are gaps between these numbers, probably indicating that Tiffany was also producing stock items intended for sale. It seems likely that these pieces were made from the middle of 1903 until June of the following year. Tiffany probably devoted his first year in this new venture, from March 1902 to the middle of 1903, to analyzing forms and techniques, and began to design seriously and create his exhibition pieces only when he was satisfied with the outcome of his experiments. Although he had been producing art objects for many years, this was his first attempt at jewelry-making, and there can be little doubt that he was more than a little intimidated by the jewelry produced by his father's company.

After his success at St. Louis, Tiffany's jewelry showed a marked evolution. Although the motifs on a few of his pieces continued to be inspired by nature, for the most part he drew increasingly from Islamic and Etruscan sources.

For a hair ornament, he combined motifs from two pieces shown at the Exposition, the dandelion and the dragonfly. Instead of depicting them separately, as he had done previously, he designed two dragonflies, each perched on a separate dandelion seed-ball[28] and presented from different perspectives. In one case, the dragonfly is placed on the side of the seed-ball with its back to the viewer; on the other, the dragonfly sits on top of a partially dispersed and/or half-eaten puff ball. Although the black-and-white photograph does not allow a precise determination, the seed-balls and insects appear to be made out of the same materials and gemstones as in the earlier pieces: small white opals on the ends of silver wire for the dandelion; opals, opalines, and demantoid garnets for the dragonflies' bodies; iridium and platinum for their wings. This piece is numbered

36

Tiffany looked to the arts of India for some of his inspiration. This corsage ornament is based on Indian forehead ornaments, not only in its conception and its substitution of silk cords for neck chains, but also in its use of seed pearls. *(Reproduced from* The International Studio, *v. 30 (November 1906), xxxii).*

Opposite, a plate from *The Journal of Indian Art*, v. III, pl. CXXII, illustrating an assortment of the type of jewelry that Tiffany collected and used for inspiration in his designs. His signature in the lower right-hand corner indicates that this plate was part of his private collection. *(Charles Hosmer Morse Museum of American Art, Winter Park, FL).*

J250 in the photographic scrapbook and would date to sometime in 1906. As a rule, Tiffany did not repeat his former designs; but in this instance, although he did re-use motifs from earlier creations, he transposed them into a three-dimensional piece of jewelry, presenting the dragonflies from two different views and the seed-ball in both its perfect and imperfect state.

Other pieces Tiffany created in his artistic jewelry department at Tiffany Furnaces included a silver collar, or band, made up of two chains with a row of 22 movable box settings in between, each section set with a topaz. The hand-made chain is composed of soldered links with no indication of a beginning or end. It passes through eyelets on each side of the rectangular sections as well as the button-like end-pieces. Instead of fastening the necklace by means of a clasp, the necklace is secured around the neck by tying the two double chains, as in Indian jewelry. In fact, this piece is very similar to an Indian necklace described in the Laurelton Hall inventory, compiled in 1919. It is listed as a "Hindoo necklace consisting of twenty two square box settings, holding cabochon moonstones strung on a double silk cord, silver button ends."[29] Tiffany adapted the Hindu necklace to his own style by substituting topaz for the moonstones and a silver chain for the silk cord. This collar or neck piece is numbered J165 and was made in 1904, probably towards the end of the year.

Approximately two years later, Tiffany redesigned the box section necklace into a more elaborate corsage ornament, based on Indian forehead ornaments. Beginning with the identical box sections, he added another

18   Louis C Tiffany

row of pearls, gemstones surrounded by seed pearls, and oval-shaped opals from which hang baroque pearls, known as hinge pearls of the dog-tooth variety. In place of the chain cords, he used silk, which is more in keeping with its Indian prototype, an example of which is illustrated in *A Golden Treasury Jewellery from the Indian Subcontinent*.[30] The design of this Tiffany corsage ornament is almost identical to the Indian piece, except for the use of drop baroque pearls instead of pearl clusters.

Tiffany collected not only books and objets d'art which he used as inspiration for his work, but also photographs, which reflected his design interests. Mention has already been made of a photograph of Queen Anne's lace and its relationship to the ornament in the St. Louis Exposition. A photograph taken from a plate in *The Journal of Indian Art*[31] (now in the Charles Hosmer Morse Museum of American Art) confirms Tiffany's interest in Indian jewelry. He must have owned similar photographs from this volume but none has survived. Tiffany even went so far as to sign the photograph, not claiming that the illustrated jewelry was his design, but rather that the photograph belonged to him. There are many photographs in the Tiffany & Co. archives that are also signed in a similar way.

The necklace in the center of the photograph from the above-mentioned Indian journal, item No. 570, is composed of numerous rows of rosettes which encircle small discs. Tiffany designed a cloak clasp, numbered J319 and dating to late 1906 or early 1907, with a similar configuration surrounding pearls; the wire rosettes are wound around a center stone.

Tiffany created several fringe necklaces along similar lines to the Etruscan-style necklace shown at St. Louis, but without the thick collar, substituting a simple chain from which filigree ornaments and gemstones were suspended. The one exhibited in the Paris Salon of 1906 was made with amethysts and jade. Like the Indian-inspired necklaces, it was tied around the neck by gold chains. Its number, J279, indicates that it was made in 1906, at about the same time as another necklace, numbered J283. This latter necklace, of openwork design with gold wirework, is enhanced by rosettes of seed pearl clusters with baroque pearl drops, the same hinge-type variety as in the box section necklace described earlier. Its oval link chain, also set with seed pearls, terminated originally at the two circular elements and tied in the Indian manner. An additional chain section with coordinating pearls and a securing clasp was added later.

Rosettes were a popular motif that Tiffany incorporated into other pieces of jewelry, such as a brooch with opals arranged in this configuration, 34 set into chrysoprase. Green from the central stone is further enhanced by four demantoid garnets in the border. This piece is numbered J350 and dates to the beginning of 1907, just before the department was consolidated at Tiffany & Co. Other pieces from this period include a pendant with a large drop baroque pearl, suspended from a grouping of filigree flowers, J353; a filigree-decorated bangle with opals and rubies, J365; and a twelve-link gold necklace, J383, in which each section was made up of concentric decorative motifs.[32]

31

The jewels Tiffany designed in 1906 and 1907 presage those he was to create at Tiffany & Co., when color became paramount. Gemstones and enameling were now carefully selected for their particular tonal effects, recalling his earlier impressionistic paintings. For the necklace numbered J380 and dating to 1907, Tiffany chose orange-hued Mexican opals and green enameling, both colors integrated by the gold background. Each of the six oval elements, as well as the heart-shaped pendant, are decorated with translucent green enameling, shaded from light to dark and slightly overlapping the central stone. The green is also repeated in truncated panels connecting the elements. In this piece, Tiffany is experimenting with a concept which is absent from his earlier jewelry, the use of geometric configurations. From the clasp, ovoid, circular and trapezoidal shapes descend to the heart-shaped pendant, repeated in the pendant drop.

39,40

Perhaps the most important extant piece of jewelry designed by Louis Tiffany is the necklace, conceived like a piece of hand-wrought Byzantine jewelry, known as the "peacock necklace" and now in the collection of the Charles Hosmer Morse Museum of American Art. It can be dated prior to 1906 since a description and an illustration of it were included in *The International Studio* article, "Louis C. Tiffany and His Work in Artistic Jewellery." Since both the obverse and reverse have been carefully finished, one must assume that it was intended for display purposes and would, therefore, have been included in the St. Louis exhibition if it had been ready. Therefore, a date of 1905 would seem probable. The central pendant of the obverse is composed of a peacock mosaic of opals with gold walls between each piece, constructed in much the same manner as cloisonné enameling. A black opal at the bottom forms the underside of the peacock's tail, while an iron-stained matrix in which opals are often found makes up the underside of the wings, striated to resemble feathers. Blue-shaded opals form the body and head as well as the sky, while mottled green and brown stones make up the background. The peacock is bordered by a ring of cabochon amethysts with a festoon chain of seed pearls and demantoid garnets skirting the top of the medallion, draping downward to a circular pendant decorated with an enameled wreath from which a ruby is suspended. The peacock motif is reiterated in the lappets, where two enameled birds face each other over a chalice with a cabochon ruby set into the rim. Their tail feathers, which rise over their heads and below their feet, are set with sapphires. Gem-set rosettes join the two peacock elements.

The peacock was one of Tiffany's favorite motifs, appearing in his stained glass windows, mosaics, favrile glass, and enamelware. Because of its radiant colorations and graceful curves, this bird was a popular theme in Art Nouveau jewelry on both sides of the Atlantic. Tiffany, however, may have chosen the motif for another reason. The peacock is the proud bird of the Orient, symbolizing immortality; this is a representation he captured in the reredos for his chapel in the 1893 World's Columbian Exposition in Chicago. A promotional booklet published by the Tiffany Glass & Decorating Company described the mosaic: "The design employed is the Vine, symbolical of the Sacrament of the Eucharist, and among these vines there are portrayed peacocks used here after the manner of the Primitive Christians, as symbolizing immortality, for it was believed in the early ages that the flesh of the peacock was incorruptible."[33] In the lappets of the "peacock necklace", as in the chapel mosaic, Tiffany depicted two peacocks facing each other. However, instead of representing clusters of grapes for the Eucharist, he depicted a chalice between the birds, and the Crown of Thorns was replaced by a laurel wreath in the drop pendant.

The reverse side of the central pendant and lappets are cloisonné 40 enameled flamingoes, their necks entwined to form an interesting design. According to Julia Munson in an interview with Hugh McKean, after Tiffany finished the peacock necklace, he thought the reverse was "too bare" and designed separate plates which could be attached to the disc.[34]

This necklace was purchased by Henry Walters sometime before 1914, since it was listed as "From the Walters Collection" in *The Art of Louis Comfort Tiffany*.[35] It was offered for sale in the auction of Mrs. Henry Walters's art collection on 25 April 1941, and catalogued as "Gold, Favrile Glass and Enamel Pectoral Ornament . . . L.C. Tiffany, New York . . . Of imaginative design, inspired by an early Scythian gold ornament. Composed of a central disc to which are attached two lappets by four rosettes; and mosaic of blue and green favrile glass and enamel, set with stones, and festooned with small pearls."[36] (The opals have been miscatalogued as favrile glass.) I have not been able to ascertain whether the necklace was in fact inspired by Scythian gold work and there is no mention in the Laurelton Hall inventory list of Tiffany's collecting such objects.

It is clear that in a few years Louis Tiffany had successfully developed his artistic concepts in the jewelry field to a mature stage. As in previous endeavors, he broadened the scope of his subject-matter and perfected his technological skills. At the same time he retained the central artistic principles that had guided him throughout his career: love of nature and endless pursuit of color. With the consolidation of his corporate position at Tiffany & Co., he was ready for a next bold move.

4

Louis Comfort Tiffany Jewelry and Tiffany & Co.

Louis Tiffany's jewelry changed dramatically once Tiffany & Co. began to manufacture his creations. His earlier pieces are freer in their interpretation of the subject and constructed in a "hand-wrought" manner, whereas the pieces made at Tiffany & Co. tend to be symmetrical and stylized. Edges are carefully finished; platinum, newly introduced to jewelry manufacture, is rendered in a fashion similar to antique work; and enameling, either translucent or transparent, complements gemstones.

After the death of Tiffany & Co.'s president, Charles Cook, on 26 January 1907, the makeup of the Board of Trustees changed radically. A special meeting was called on 15 February to elect a new slate of officers. John C. Moore, who had been first vice-president since 1902, was elected to succeed Cook and Louis Tiffany became first vice-president and assistant treasurer.[1] On 3 May, Tiffany & Co. bought the enameling and jewelry division of Tiffany Furnaces.

It is interesting to explore just why Louis Tiffany felt he could direct his father's company to manufacture the jewelry and enamels that he had heretofore been producing at Tiffany Furnaces and retailing at Tiffany & Co. By now, Tiffany was a major shareholder in Tiffany & Co.; in fact, he held a controlling financial interest. However, this had been true ever since the death of his father in 1902. We may ask why he waited until 1907 to reorganize his enamel and jewelry division within Tiffany & Co.

The answer can be found in the personality of Charles Cook, who had started working for the company in 1847 as a cash boy[2] and had risen to become president in 1902. It seems logical to assume that, after a 55-year tenure with the company, he would have found it difficult to change the firm's business direction and practises. Louis Tiffany waited until after Cook's death to announce the new move, at a time when he would have the support of the new president, the son of the man who had been the young Louis Tiffany's mentor in his formative years.

With Cook gone, Tiffany was able to exert full artistic leadership, taking over the responsibility that Paulding Farnham had had since the late

1890s. It was not long before Farnham left the company and moved to California. In the absence of precise information, one can only speculate that there was no room for these two extraordinarily talented artists in the same company. Louis Tiffany, of course, had the upper hand and did not hesitate to use his advantage to forge ahead with his artistic agenda.

The minutes of the Tiffany & Co. board meeting on 3 May 1907 record the following arrangement:

The Furnaces [*i.e.*, Tiffany Furnaces] for some time past has maintained a special department for the manufacture of jewelry in combination of precious stones, gold, silver and other metals, both plain and enameled, and the Company [*i.e.*, Tiffany & Co.] has acted as sole selling agent for articles so manufactured. The Furnaces agrees to sell and the Company agrees to purchase all stock, assets and good will of the said department, including articles manufactured and in process of manufacture, samples, models, metals, precious stones, safes, fixtures, tools, etc; for the sum of $35,000.

The document continues, ''. . . the Furnaces expressly stipulates and agrees that it will not anytime in the future maintain a similar department or engage in the manufacture of jewelry of any kind or description, or in enameling of precious metals for any purpose whatsoever.'' The department had actually changed hands on 1 April, but the disposition of funds was not finalized until this board meeting. The agreement further stipulated that all expenses accrued until 3 May would be paid by Tiffany & Co.[3] These amounted to an additional sum of $328.97. From this point until the department closed in 1933, Tiffany & Co. manufactured all of Louis Tiffany's jewelry and enamelware, with the exception of desk sets and complementary items, often highlighted with enameling, which were produced at Tiffany Furnaces. (Such items will not be discussed in this book.)

A special department was set up on the sixth floor of the Tiffany & Co. store at 37th Street and Fifth Avenue for the manufacture of Louis's jewelry and enamels. (The new department displaced the workshops for clocks, case goods, and leather goods, as well as several storerooms.) The finished pieces were offered for sale on the ground floor along with other Tiffany Furnaces and Tiffany Studios items, such as leaded glass lamps, favrile glass, ceramics and desk sets. Cornelius Quinn represented the company as salesman.

Dr. Parker McIlhinny and Julia Munson, who had been working at Tiffany Furnaces, were transferred to the new department at Tiffany & Co. Munson worked on the sixth floor, where she was assisted by Donna Phelps Bain. The following year, James J. Patterson, who had been a floor boy, and John J. O'Hara, who also worked in the clock shop, began working in the department; Susie Shroeder Hayes joined the company in 1912.

Miss Munson received $30 weekly in 1908, and her salary was raised to $40 on 17 January 1909.[4] She remained at the head of the department until she resigned on 3 February 1914 to marry Frederic Fairchild Sherman. Thomas B. Winship joined the department on 5 February 1914 and was appointed director of the shop. He remained in this position only until 20 April when Meta K. Overbeck joined the company and assumed charge of the department, at a salary of $35 a week.

In 1915 and 1916, only Meta Overbeck and Susie Hayes were working in Louis Tiffany's jewelry and enameling department, together with an apprentice, A. Uhl, who remained for one year. In 1917, Susie Hayes left and Isabel Coles joined the company, remaining until 1925. In 1918, Freida Schroeder, who had worked in the fifth-floor shop that produced jewelry for Tiffany & Co., was first transferred to the sixth floor, and then to the watch shop. On 18 August 1919, Harriet Van Tassel, who had also been working in the fifth-floor shop, entered the department. In 1920, Minnie Rackle, Dorothy Armbruster, who was the daughter of Tiffany salesman Henry Armbruster, and Herbert B. Winship all joined the department but left within the year, Winship to take a position with Krementz & Co. in Newark, New Jersey.

From 1920 until the department closed in 1933, Meta Overbeck worked with Harriet Van Tassel. Other women employed in the department during the 1920s included Elsie Moglia, nee Datesman, Miss E. E. Biggs, Miss C. M. Henry, and Miss N. K. Barton. Overbeck remained in charge of the department until after Tiffany's death in 1933; on July 1st of that year she was transferred to jewelry stock.[5]

The department remained small, ranging in size from two employees in the first and final three years to a maximum of six in 1920, with the average somewhere between three and four. It functioned for 26 years, employing a total of nineteen people, thirteen women and only six men.

Tiffany's tradition of hiring women predates his association with Tiffany & Co. As early as 1892, he employed six women at his glass works in Corona, New York, a number that by 1894 had grown to 35, while twenty additional ladies worked in the embroidery department. Tiffany turned to the local YWCA, Cooper Union, and the School of Applied Design to meet his growing staff needs.[6] He relied upon the expertise that women could bring to these special crafts since, as he felt, their hands were ideally suited to handling the intricate patterns involved in delicate work. In an article on this subject, Polly King wrote in 1894, "In the field of pure ornament and pure color, for dexterity of handling and execution of detail, women are unsurpassed in this work . . ."[7]

The women Tiffany entrusted to head departments, such as Mrs. O. F. M. Hardoncourt in the embroidery department and Mrs. Clara Driscoll in the stained glass window department, trained directly under him. Every design had to be approved by Tiffany before it was executed. This rule also held true for the jewelry and enameling division. The Tiffany & Co. 1909 *Blue Book* clearly stipulated that each article was "Designed and made under the personal supervision of Louis C. Tiffany."[8] Tiffany would roughly sketch an idea on paper, then his designers, either Miss Munson or Miss Overbeck, would make a watercolor cartoon. After that, a wax model would be executed over which the framework for the jewel was constructed. At various times during the development of a piece of jewelry, Tiffany would make recommendations. Since he was involved in so many varied areas, he came to rely increasingly on his staff to carry out his ideas. According to Charles DeKay, "Mr. Tiffany has his helpers so well trained that he needs to devote but a few hours a day to enamels and jewelry."[9]

Although no records exist to explain why Tiffany hired predominantly women in his enameling and jewelry division, his experience in the glass division probably influenced this decision. Cecilia Waern, writing in 1897, tells us that Tiffany apprenticed young men to learn the skills of glassmaking; however, his workmen, objecting to his hiring so many apprentices, called a strike. Tiffany reacted to this by letting all the men go and replacing them with women. Waern summarized Tiffany's stance by concluding that young women had learned "to use their eyes and their fingers in certain ways" and were capable of producing glass when trained under his direction.[10]

After 1907, all of Louis Tiffany's jewelry made at Tiffany & Co. bears the Tiffany & Co. stamp, either impressed into the mounting or on an attached plaque. Each piece was hand-crafted, based on the original rendering; nothing was stamped out or cast. This craftsmanship ideal was followed at the time by Arts and Crafts designers in England and in Boston, and it had been the tradition in ancient civilizations, a source Tiffany often turned to for inspiration. Each jewel thus became a unique example of Tiffany's art. The 1909 Tiffany *Blue Book* stated, "No pieces duplicated;"[11] this was amended in the 1912 edition to read, "The finer pieces will not be duplicated."[12] Small articles, such as simple bar pins or scarf pins, embellished with a favrile glass beetle, were made in multiples, but they were still considered works of art. According to Julia Munson, "Every piece was made to stand perfectly on its own and last, and even improve with time."[13] After handling a fair amount of Louis's jewelry, one can feel a certain "specialness" about each piece, clearly treated by Tiffany as an individual creation.

Although one can generally categorize Tiffany's jewelry oeuvre according to two major areas of influence, naturalism and historicism, it becomes apparent under close examination that many other influences are reflected in his work. Just when one feels comfortable arranging his work into acceptable categories, a piece appears that was obviously designed by Tiffany but does not fit into those patterns.

Unlike the Tiffany & Co. practice of using the finest gemstones in jewelry, Louis would select a stone not for its intrinsic value, but for its coloristic qualities. According to Munson again, "Our idea was to take an inexpensive stone and bring out its natural beauty and luster by echoing its feeling in its treatment. Each piece had a name and a personality."[14] Tiffany & Co. preferred setting stones in a prong or claw mounting and, in the last quarter of the 19th century, perfected the "Tiffany setting" in which prongs held the gem away from the mounting, thereby allowing light to shine through and enhance the brilliance of the stone. In contrast, Louis Tiffany, for the most part, mounted his stones in a closed collet setting that encircled the gemstone and held it in place, a technique based on medieval and Renaissance jewelry.

The first recorded source for Louis Comfort Tiffany's jewelry made at Tiffany & Co. is the 1909 Tiffany *Blue Book*.[15] The catalogue is arranged alphabetically with Louis's jewelry listed under "Tiffany Art Jewelry", a department which was clearly designated as separate from Tiffany & Co. stock. The listing described the jewelry as follows: "Among the features of this work are the remarkable color effects obtained in the combinations of gold and enamel with precious and semi-precious stones." Enameling complemented colored gemstones. When precious stones such as diamonds were used, they were considered part of the coloristic tableau and contrasted with other colored gemstones, as is apparent on a necklace in the Walters Art Gallery in which canary diamonds are juxtaposed with zircons.

Tiffany considered white diamonds too monochromatic for his taste, and rarely used them. His early experience as an impressionist painter continued to influence his later creations, especially jewelry.

Tiffany & Co. offered a variety of Louis Tiffany's items, including handbags, set with opals, demantoid garnets, and amethysts; belts of handwoven silk with enameled and jeweled buckles; hair ornaments and hat pins, enameled and set with precious and semi-precious stones. Bracelets were enameled and set with turquoise, corals, amethysts, and demantoid garnets. Necklaces were composed of sapphires, pearls, opals, tourmalines, and other colored gemstones, and brooches of sapphires, opals, peridots, amethysts, and tourmalines. Collars and pendants were made up of a variety of precious and colored gemstones. Prices for these items ranged from $17.00 for a hat pin to $3,500 for an elaborate necklace.

One of the earliest known examples of Louis Comfort Tiffany jewelry produced at Tiffany & Co. is a pink pearl brooch. Although stamped with

42

the Tiffany & Co. mark, it is closely related to those works executed at Tiffany Furnaces. Its organic and naturalistic feeling relates it more closely to brooches Tiffany exhibited in the 1904 Louisiana Purchase Exposition in St. Louis, in which stones are partially concealed within enameled settings of leaves and berries.[16] The pearls in this brooch are set into silver, mounted onto a gold backing. They resemble rocks embedded in sand at low tide; the water swirling around them is portrayed in sea green enamel. This brooch has been assigned the number J286 in a photographic scrapbook in the Tiffany & Co. archives. Two necklaces, executed at Tiffany Furnaces, are numbered J282 and J380 respectively in a scrapbook. The first can be dated to 1906 through an illustration in the November issue of *The International Studio*,[17] while the second, which is part of the collection of the Virginia Museum of Fine Arts, can be dated to early 1907, up to the time when the jewelry and enameling department became part of Tiffany & Co. Since brooch J268 was given a number which falls between those pieces executed at Tiffany Furnaces, I speculate that it was finished just after the department was consolidated at Tiffany & Co.

There are two photographic scrapbooks of Louis Tiffany's jewelry designs in the Tiffany & Co. archives. Each item illustrated in these books has been assigned a production number, prefixed with either the letter ''J'', ''T'' or ''F''. After studying these photographs and comparing them to pieces available today, I have come to the conclusion that those pieces with numbers bearing the letter ''J'' were designed while Julia Munson was in charge of the jewelry department; those with ''T'' were produced from 5 February to 20 April 1914, during Thomas B. Winship's short directorship; and those with ''F'' date from April 1914 until the department closed in 1933, during Meta Overbeck's tenure. This is substantiated from a scrapbook of jewelry drawings, at the Charles Hosmer Morse Museum of American Art, which were executed by Meta Overbeck. Each drawing in this book has been given a production number, similar to those in the two photographic albums, prefixed by an ''F''.

Since Louis Tiffany had to approve all preliminary sketches, there is a certain stylistic similarity among the work of his three designers. All three designers emphasize impressionistic color tonalities in their work, and draw upon nature, exotic Eastern sources and ancient historical periods for inspiration, as is true of all of Tiffany's oeuvre. However, when you contrast the work of the three designers, certain distinctive features become evident. Julia Munson's jewelry generally features simpler mountings, the pendants and brooches set with a single stone, surrounded by either enameling or filigree work. Gemstones are rarely faceted and are more likely to be cut en cabochon. Her pendant chains are designed along traditional lines with interconnecting links. Since Thomas B. Winship remained in the department for such a short time, his creations tend to be similar to Munson's. Like his predecessor, he continued to use moonstones set in platinum mounts. However, when Meta Overbeck took over the department, Tiffany's jewelry assumed a more elaborate appearance. Colored gemstones are faceted or carved, and settings become more complex. Single gemstones are now placed within naturalistically treated mountings of vines and leaves arranged with less emphasis on symmetry. Color tones are still based on impressionistic effects, but with the advent of the Art Deco period, brighter colors begin to emerge. In general terms, Tiffany's earlier jewelry, designed while Munson was director of the department, is simpler, with less emphasis on ornate mountings. Once Overbeck took over the department his jewelry evolved into more elaborate and colorful compositions.

As we know, Louis Tiffany had a large collection of objets d'art which he used in his search for motifs. In 1919, when he presented his home to the Tiffany Foundation, an inventory was compiled of all the items in his house. Among them were several cases of jewelry located in the second-floor gallery. One, mounted on the wall, contained an assortment of jewelry: Babylonian necklaces, Egyptian mummy bead necklaces and bracelets, Tyrian necklaces, an African neckband, Spanish earrings, Greek gold earrings from the 4th century BC, Italian silver cross pendants from the 17th century, Hindu necklaces and a filigree neck ornament, a Chinese filigree hairpin, an Albanian buckle, and arm bands from Benin.[18] Just as Edward Moore had used his extensive collection as source material for his silver designs, Louis Tiffany transposed motifs from his small jewelry collection onto his jeweled creations.

Egypt was a source of inspiration Tiffany turned to repeatedly throughout his career. His earlier works, such as bronze inkstands, wooden humidors, and the Gould Lamp, incorporated Egyptian scarabs as a decorative motif. These were carried over into his jewelry, in which they became dominant images. He was not the only designer of his time to use this ancient Egyptian symbol. An article in *The Jewelers' Circular-Weekly* in 1908 cites the scarab as a popular motif, which "the jeweler is resuscitating",[19] most likely in response to Sir Flinders Petrie's archaeological excavations in the first decade of the century.

Along with Louis's gemstone and enameled jewelry advertised in the 1909 Tiffany & Co. *Blue Book*, a selection of favrile glass beetle jewelry was also offered. (Although based on the Egyptian scarab, Tiffany preferred to call them beetles.) Such items as belt pins, belts, hat pins, lorgnon chains, necklaces and lavallières, scarf pins, sleeve links, studs and collar buttons, and watch guards were offered at prices from $4.50 for a scarf pin to $105 for a belt; the following year, necklaces and lavallières became more elaborate and were offered at prices from $20 to $225. Pendants were added in 1910 and charms in 1911. The actual beetles were made in shades of red or blue and were available in various sizes,

The favrile glass shapes that Tiffany used in his "beetle" jewelry were stamped in a tile, then cut out and set into 18-karat gold mountings. *(Collection of Jason Ellman)*.

A pair of cufflinks and two scarf pins mounted with Tiffany favrile glass beetles. *(Collection of Gladys and Robert Koch).*

The Egyptian necklace of dried scarabs in Tiffany's collection (Ill. 45) may have influenced the arrangement of the beetles in the necklace opposite. The buckle is set with a favrile glass beetle, surrounded by enameling. *(Collection of Lillian Nassau).*

depending upon their particular use. They were stamped into a glass tile, and then cut out and set into 18 karat gold mountings. The beetle was set into a bezel mounting, the back totally enclosed, similar to the Egyptian manner of mounting scarabs in a metal frame or funda in order to protect their edges from injury. Once mounted, they were either placed on top of a hat pin, suspended from chains in a necklace, or enframed within a spiral motif.

Subsequent *Blue Books* offered these items until 1914, which would indicate that most of them were created while Julia Munson was in charge of the department. One of the photographic scrapbook illustrates several pieces of Tiffany's beetle jewelry, the numbers prefixed with the letter ''F''. Most of these numbers range from F87 to F118, during the first year that Meta Overbeck was director of the department. Although Tiffany discontinued making favrile glass beetle jewelry, the interest in it continued to spread throughout the country, perhaps spurred on by his example. An article in *The Jewelers'-Circular Weekly* of 1916 proclaimed ''the latest thing in ornamental wear . . . one piece of jewelry particularly are they copying—the 'Scarab'.''[20]

Although it is not known whether Tiffany chose the scarab because of its ancient symbolism (representing resurrection and immortality), he was certainly interested in its shape and its iridescence from a design standpoint. In ancient Egypt, scarabs were used as religious talismans, reproduced on jewelry, and made up the upper side of a seal stone. According to Percy Newberry, the scarabs on these seals ranged in size from $\frac{1}{5}$ inch to 4 or 5 inches in length. The most common size is $\frac{3}{4}$ inch long by $\frac{1}{2}$ inch wide by $\frac{1}{4}$ inch high.[21] Although it is not known whether Tiffany had access to this book, he was most likely aware of the general sizes of these articles. The beetles in one of his necklaces measure 1 inch by $\frac{1}{2}$ inch wide, whereas smaller beetles in other jewelry came in sizes $\frac{5}{8}$ inch long by $\frac{1}{4}$ inch wide.

Among the Egyptian objects in Tiffany's collection were ''eleven Egyptian mummy bead necklaces of glass and glazed pottery; Egyptian (repro) necklace with five pendant loops, small gold beads, pearls, and pendant, earring to match; two Egyptian mummy bracelets, large red pottery beads attached to reed wrist bands with cord lashings; and an Egyptian horse ornament, crescent of boars tusks, metal center and chalcedony bead pendant.''[22] The Egyptian (repro) necklace was made up of dried scarabs,[23] which were popular in the late 19th century. The iridescent blue scarabs closely resemble the colorations on Tiffany beetle jewelry. The style of the necklace with its scarab pendants suspended from a beaded chain is similar to Tiffany's favrile glass beetle necklace and may have served as a prototype. Both necklaces are reminiscent of an Egyptian example, dating from the Fourth Dynasty, in which a row of 50 gold scarabs are suspended from two gold wires.[24]

Along with his favrile glass beetles, Tiffany set selected pieces of his glass tiles into silver mounts, marked "Tiffany & Co." *(Collection of Gladys and Robert Koch).*

Louis Tiffany would also have been aware of a scarabei hand mirror,[25] its back embellished with seven scarabs, that Tiffany & Co. exhibited at the 1893 World's Columbian Exposition held in Chicago (contributed by John T. Curran, director of the silverware division, among other items in the display). Since Louis Tiffany shared space with his father's company at this exhibition, he was undoubtedly familiar with the items shown.

Howard Carter's discovery of Tutankhamun's tomb in 1922, and the press coverage this generated, spawned a renewed interest in Egypt. Such Parisian jewelers as Cartier and Van Cleef & Arpels created elaborate precious stone jewelry, featuring pictorial Egyptian motifs based on Art Deco designs. Louis Tiffany interpreted this latest resurgence of Egyptomania by resurrecting his scarab, but instead of using favrile glass, he turned to gemstones and enameling. The scarab became grander, depicted with wings, similar to ancient Egyptian pectoral ornaments placed on the breast of the deceased. These articles were produced under the direction of Meta Overbeck. A drawing in her jewelry drawing scrapbook, page 12, depicts a necklace in which the central scarab, made up of a blue stone which could be lapis lazuli, is flanked by outstretched wings and suspended from a bead chain. Beads were popular in ancient Egyptian jewelry, a decorative motif that Tiffany incorporated in his later Egyptian revival jewelry. 47

The scarab necklace is numbered F5150 and dates to *c.* 1923, about the same time another necklace was produced. The chain on the latter necklace is made up of alternating beads of jade, lapis, coral and gold. Each bead is connected by a pigtail chain clearly visible on the suspending tassels. The pendant represents some type of beetle, but not the Egyptian winged scarab in which the wings flare out from the insect's body and over its head. Instead, the stylized wings in plique-à-jour enamel begin in the area between the head and the body, spreading out and away from the body to the lower section. Turquoise, lapis and jade make up the insect. Here again, Tiffany is juxtaposing colors to give a harmonious effect to the overall design. On another necklace, amber, carnelian, garnet, opal, orange and blue sapphire, spessartite garnet and tourmaline beads lead the viewer's eye to the main attraction—a beautifully faceted alexandrite set into a restrained Art Nouveau mount. Each gemstone bead is connected by a pigtail chain. 44

Other insects intrigued Tiffany besides the beetle. At both the St. Louis exhibition in 1904 and the 1906 Paris Salon, Tiffany exhibited a dragonfly hair ornament, an adaptation of which he produced at Tiffany & Co. and offered in the *Blue Books* from 1914 until 1918 at a price of $300. The entry describes it only as set with opals when in fact the body of the dragonfly is composed of black opals with demantoid garnets between platinum filigree wings.

At the 1904 St. Louis exhibition, Tiffany showed a dragonfly hair ornament (see p. 79) which was similar to this brooch, made up of black opals, demantoid garnets, platinum and gold. (Private collection).

In the revival of Egyptian-inspired jewelry that followed the opening of Tutankhamun's tomb in 1922, Tiffany created many pieces in this style, such as the necklace above made up of gold, jade, lapis lazuli and coral beaded chain. The body of the insect is in turquoise, lapis and jade with plique-à-jour enameling.

Tiffany used platinum in his jewelry creations artfully as filigree, in a manner familiar from ancient jewelry. For the Columbian Exposition Chapel, he created a pair of altar candlesticks, fashioning the gilded metal into filigree work. Favrile glass jewels were embedded into the design to resemble gemstones. He re-created a similar effect in the altar cross that he made later to replace the lost original. Here, he used favrile glass colored much like moonstones.

Tiffany used moonstones in many of his jewelry designs, most likely because they reminded him of the translucent glass he had been creating at the Tiffany Studios. Due to the pale color of moonstones, a silver-colored metal was considered more suitable for mounting. After the turn of the century when platinum became more readily available, jewelers used this new metal to set a variety of gemstones, such as diamonds, which had heretofore been set in silver mounts. Tiffany preferred this new metal to enhance the beauty of his moonstone jewelry.

In the case of a moonstone and sapphire brooch, analytical testing showed that the mounting was made up of palladium, while the filigree between the moonstones was platinum. The pin and gold balls tested 18 karat gold. If the necklace in the same group as the brooch were analyzed, it would prove to be made of the same elements, palladium mounts with platinum filigree. The pendant in this necklace is similar in design to item number J2647 in the photographic scrapbook. It would therefore have been made while Julia Munson was in charge of the department and its numbering would date it to c. 1912–13.

46

Articles of platinum jewelry were first advertised in the *Blue Book* in 1912, which would support this date. Bandeaux of platinum filigree work, enameled and set with moonstones, sapphires and coral, were offered from $225 to $1,000. A head ornament, illustrated in the photographic scrapbook in the Tiffany archives, is set with moonstones. This article is numbered T27 and is one of the few items designed by Thomas Winship. It can be dated to 1914, just a year after Tiffany's Egyptian party, which at the time was touted as the most lavish costume fete ever seen in New York City. One can imagine this elaborate head ornament, with its roundels covering each ear from which emanate four encircling straps, gracing the head of a beautifully attired woman at one of Tiffany's extravaganzas.

Among those items inventoried at Laurelton Hall are several examples of filigree work. They include a group of European silver filigree buttons; an antique Hindu silver filigree neck ornament, set with turquoise and other stones; a buckle of similar workmanship; a silver plaited cord and filigree bead necklace; an Albanian silver filigree buckle; and a filigree silver ornament. These articles are similar to jewelry that Edward C. Moore collected and which he bequeathed to The Metropolitan Museum of Art. One such necklace, a 19th-century example from Yemen and illustrated facing page 128 in *Islamic Jewelry in The Metropolitan Museum of Art*, is made up of pendant elements with identical filigree work that Louis Tiffany was to use in his jewelry designs.[26]

In the necklace opposite, Tiffany has characteristically suspended the moonstone pendant from a filigree platinum chain. *(Private collection)*.

Another term for this type of work is *cannetille*, a popular technique in France in the first quarter of the 19th century. Two thin wires are twisted together in a rope-like manner, then fashioned into rosettes, scrolls or beads of coiled wire.[27] An example of this type of work can be seen on the corners of a Tiffany brooch J2335, of about 1912, made up of twisted wire, coiled within oval decorative motifs. The circular platinum configurations at the corners contrast with the intervening gold parallel bars.

The center of this brooch, dated to c. 1910, is a sapphire, highlighted with plique-à-jour enameling. *(Collection of Gladys and Robert Koch)*.

Tiffany's filigree jewelry was designed while Julia Munson was in charge of the department. This technique can also be seen on designs that incorporate plique-à-jour enameling in the open spaces of the filigree work. Brooches and pendants of this type usually contain a central stone, such as an opal, hanging freely within a wreath of plique-à-jour enameling. The green, mauve and pale blue color tones of the opal in one pendant are reiterated in the surrounding enameling in a manner similar to Tiffany's earlier Impressionistic paintings. This pendant is numbered J1320 and dates to *c.* 1910; three brooches of the same type are numbered J1413, J1475, and J1852 respectively, and are of about the same date.

When Meta Overbeck assumed control of the department, she continued to produce jewelry with filigree work. Her first known example is a

63

The watch bracelet Tiffany designed for a Patek Philippe movement. *(Collection of Neil Lane and Robert Rehnert).*

Faceted stones appeared in Tiffany's jewellery after Meta Overbeck became director of the department. This necklace is set with tourmalines with plique-à-jour enameling. *(Private collection. Courtesy Ira Simon).*

tourmaline necklace number F697, dating to 1914, that incorporates panels of filigree design with plique-à-jour enameling. The gemstones are faceted, Overbeck's preference over Munson's choice of polished stones.

A watch was made a few years later, in 1917. The band is composed of parallel bands in six sections, each panel made up of filigree work. The patterning is continued around the Patek Philippe dial. Except for a brief time during the 1870s when Tiffany & Co. maintained a watch factory in Geneva, the firm did not make movements for the watches they retailed. Usually, a movement was ordered, and the watch case was decorated by the firm's design staff. In the above example, Louis Tiffany would have either ordered the movement or selected one from Tiffany's inventory.

Tiffany preferred gemstones that were either opaque or translucent. Turquoise, jade, carnelian, lapis, moonstones, and opals were chosen either for their denseness or their ability to filter light. Emphasis was placed on color, typical of all Tiffany's work.

Opaque stones feature deep color tones. Their dense qualities do not allow light to penetrate, an effect Tiffany was striving for in some of his jewelry to contrast with stones that were translucent. In a bib style necklace, *c.* 1910, sections of jade alternate with rosettes of pearls in a manner similar to his earlier "hand-wrought" jewelry. The deep green shade contrasts with the lustrous colors in the pearls. Turquoise was another of Tiffany's preferred stones, which he incorporated into bead and pendant necklaces. In one example, pebble-shaped beads of turquoise, lapis and carnelian are interspersed with hammered gold beads. This necklace is similar to J1870 in the photographic scrapbook and dates to *c.* 1910. For these necklaces, Tiffany turned to Eastern influences, especially India and Tibet, where such stones as lapis, turquoise and carnelian were always favored. In the East, stones were assigned talismanic powers; in Tibet, for example, turquoise was considered to have protective value. At the turn of the century, this stone was also associated with good fortune. On another necklace, a polished turquoise is set into a rectangular plaque with complementary opaque enameling surrounding the stone. Similar colorations are continued on the link chain with small stones interspersed with gold enameled fan-shaped plaques. These small plaques were included on trace chains as on the above example, with or without coordinating stones; interspersed with moonstones dangling on fringe necklaces; contrasted with pearl rosettes, either in the form of pendant drop earrings or on necklaces (number J860); and incorporated into brooches with an opaque stone between two fan-shaped terminals.[28] They were first conceived while Munson was in charge of the department but their popularity continued after she left.

50

53

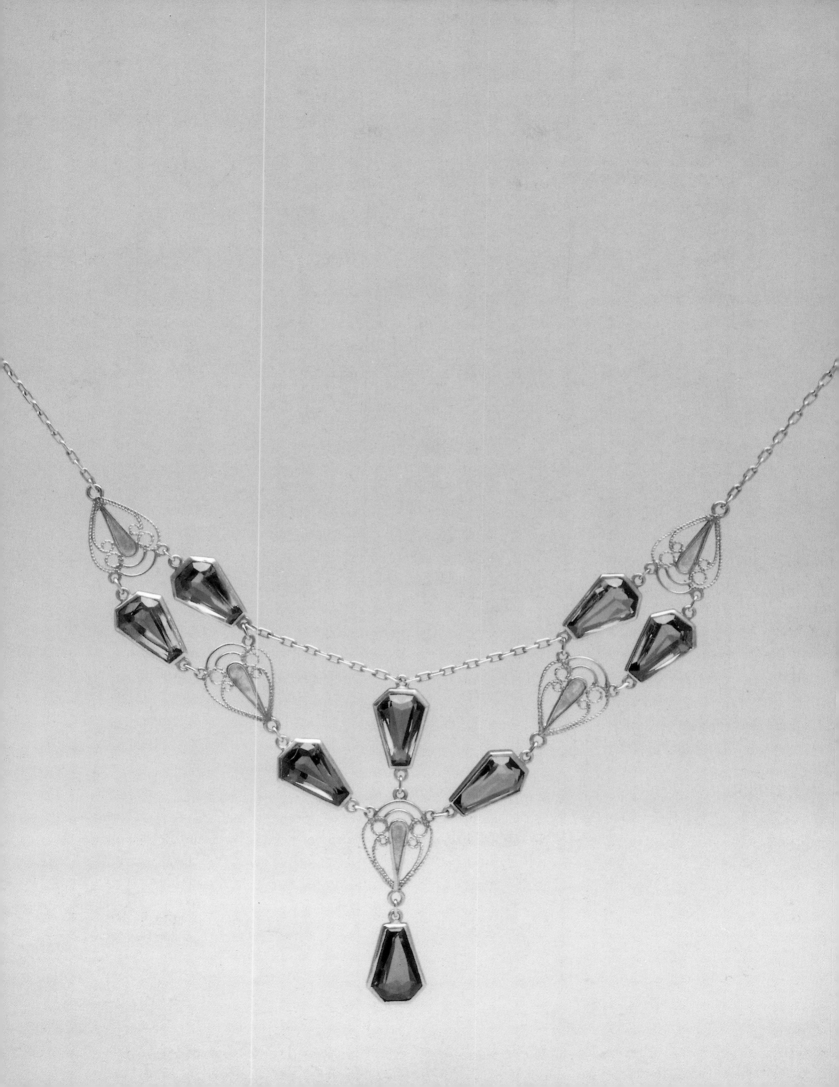

A later bib necklace than the example shown in Ill. 38. Here too the rosettes are studded with seed pearls, but in place of baroque pearl drops Tiffany designed oval jade drops. (Private collection).

42. Tiffany used diamonds only if they complemented other gemstones within his coloristic tableau, as on this platinum necklace, with a 37-carat zircon and canary diamonds, zircons, amethysts and demantoid garnets. The necklace was a wedding present from her husband to Ellen DuPont Wheelwright in 1915. (Walters Art Gallery, Baltimore, MD).

43. Tiffany created many jewels with favrile glass beetles, such as this necklace in which three drop pendants are suspended from a double row of beetles. *(Private collection)*.

44. This necklace pendant is made up of two gold Egyptian cobra symbols placed on each side of a polished lapis with a gold scarab underneath. *(Private collection, by courtesy of Macklowe Gallery & Modernism, New York)*.

45. This Egyptian necklace of dried scarabs was part of Louis Tiffany's collection at Laurelton Hall and probably served as inspiration for his beetle jewelry. *(Lillian Nassau Ltd.)*.

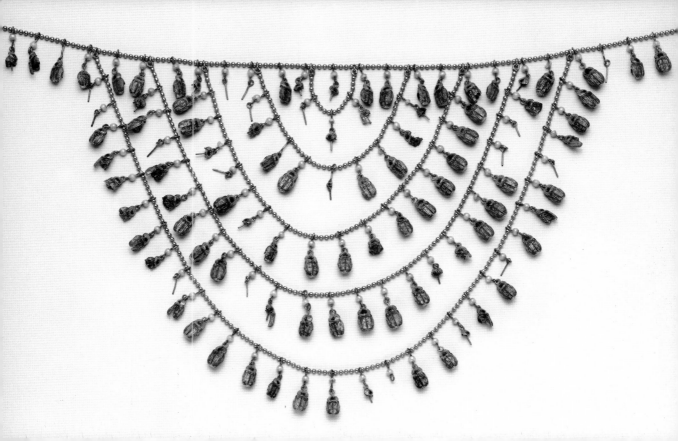

46. Tiffany set his moonstone jewelry in platinum, often using Montana sapphires as complementary stones, as in this necklace. *(Private collection).* The two brooches also contain 18-karat gold. *(Private collection and Collection of Neil Lane and Robert Rehnert).*

47. This page from a sketchbook used by Meta K. Overbeck after she took over management of the jewelry department in 1914 shows an assortment of Tiffany's jewelry designs, including two Egyptian Revival necklaces. *(Charles Hosmer Morse Museum of American Art, Winter Park, FL).*

48. A platinum bracelet set with oval and round moonstones and Montana sapphires, which was probably made while Julia Munson was director of Tiffany's jewelry department prior to 1914. *(Macklowe Gallery & Modernism, New York).*

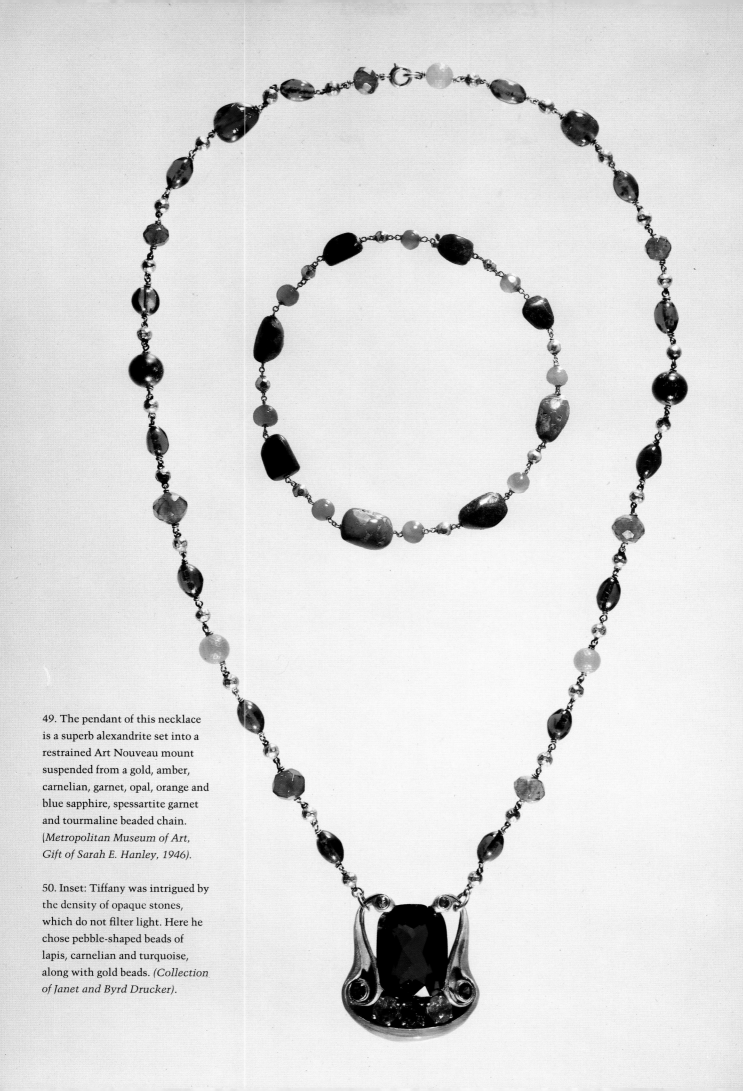

49. The pendant of this necklace is a superb alexandrite set into a restrained Art Nouveau mount suspended from a gold, amber, carnelian, garnet, opal, orange and blue sapphire, spessartite garnet and tourmaline beaded chain. *(Metropolitan Museum of Art, Gift of Sarah E. Hanley, 1946).*

50. Inset: Tiffany was intrigued by the density of opaque stones, which do not filter light. Here he chose pebble-shaped beads of lapis, carnelian and turquoise, along with gold beads. *(Collection of Janet and Byrd Drucker).*

53. A polished turquoise is set into a pendant with complementary enameling; the coloring continues onto the fan-shaped plaques and turquoise sections on the chain. *(Collection of Gladys and Robert Koch).*

51. Tiffany used fan-shaped plaques as elements in earrings, brooches and necklaces, where they were interspersed with seed pearl rosettes. *(Collection of Natalie A. Helander).*

52. Tiffany created simple fringe necklaces that were reminiscent of Greek jewelry. This enameled gold necklace, for example, is set with sapphires, *(Private collection).*

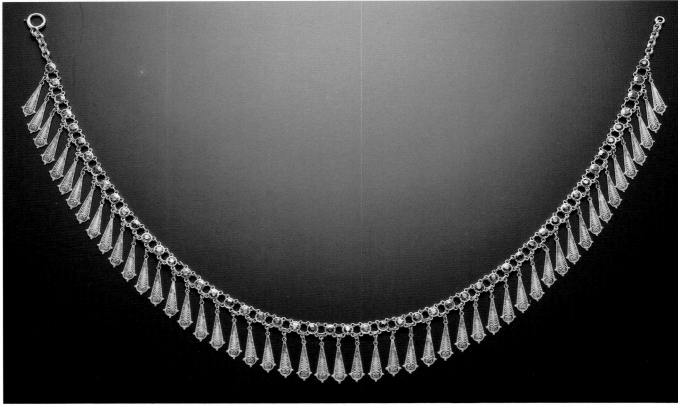

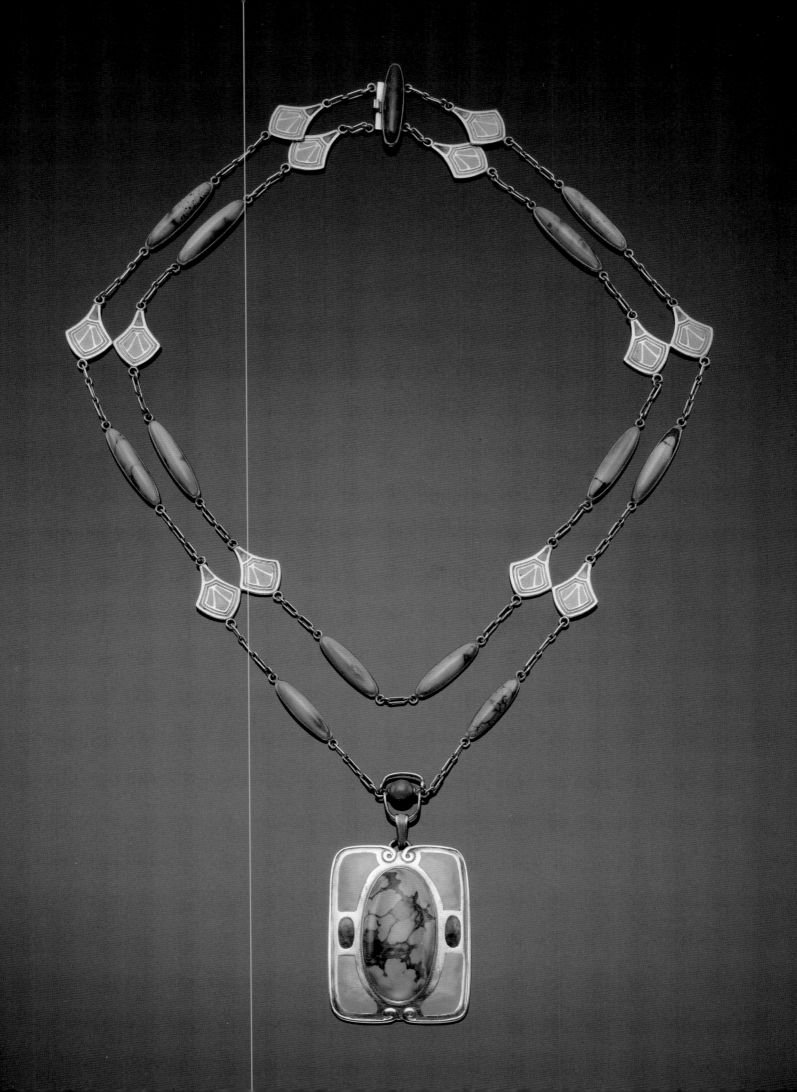

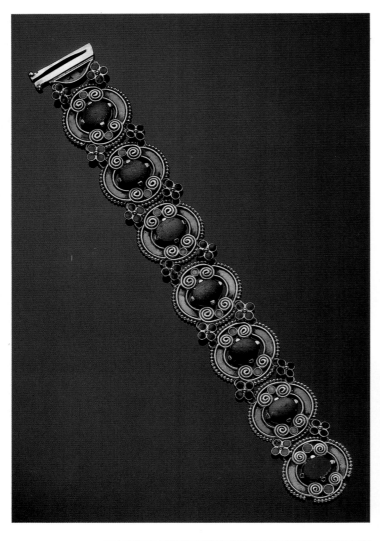

54. The filigree decoration on this gold and enamel bracelet, set with lapis, resembles Celtic designs found on jewelry in Saxon graves in England. *(Collection of Gladys and Robert Koch).*

55. A ring on which grape leaves encircle a tourmaline. On the shank, sapphires are intermixed with grape clusters. *(Charles Hosmer Morse Museum of American Art, Winter Park, FL).*

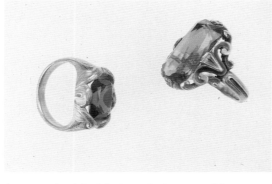

56. Two gold rings in a restrained Art Nouveau design, one with a citrine and the other with a tourmaline. *(Charles Hosmer Morse Museum of American Art, Winter Park, FL).*

57. A somewhat formally conceived necklace with a black opal. The ring is also set with a black opal. *(Collection of Gladys and Robert Koch).*

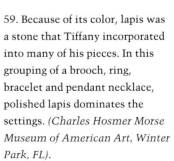

58. Oval and square lapis buttons are accentuated with green and blue enameling on this gold bracelet.

59. Because of its color, lapis was a stone that Tiffany incorporated into many of his pieces. In this grouping of a brooch, ring, bracelet and pendant necklace, polished lapis dominates the settings. *(Charles Hosmer Morse Museum of American Art, Winter Park, FL).*

60. The blue shades in the rectangular-cut aquamarine are repeated in the enameled forget-me-nots with small opals in their pistils. *(Private collection, courtesy of Ira Simon).*

61. Since opals are translucent, the wirework under the stone is visible, which creates an effect similar to plique-à-jour enameling. *(Charles Hosmer Morse Museum of American Art, Winter Park, FL).*

62. The colors of the suspended opal in this pendant (*c.* 1910) are repeated in the surrounding plique-à-jour enameling. *(Private collection).*

63. Two brooches of around 1910 made of a central stone surrounded by filigree with plique-à-jour enameling; the oval is a tourmaline, the other a zircon and opals. *(Charles Hosmer Morse Museum of American Art, Winter Park, FL).*

64. The boulder opal in this brooch is still in its iron-stained matrix, an unusual material for jewelry. Tobacco-like leaves envelop the stone, ending in stylized flowers set with seven yellow beryls. *(Collection of Neil Lane and Robert Rehnert).*

65. Tiffany designed gold brooches in a variety of colored gemstones. In four of these examples, the stones are surrounded by enameled leaves and flowers, typical of his work between 1915 and 1925. The fifth brooch is decorated with filigree, similar to his moonstone jewelry. The stones from top to bottom are lapis lazuli, amethyst, brown jade, Ceylon sapphires, Ceylon sapphires and green tourmaline. *(Private collection).*

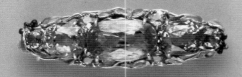

66. A necklace made of 24-karat gold pellets which have been hammered into organic shapes. It was set with a pink pearl and a baroque pearl, but the latter has been replaced. *(Collection of the author).*

67. The simplicity of this pendant/brooch conceals the intricacies of its manufacture. The faceted amethyst is set into a platinum box mounting. Smaller amethysts, cut into hexagonal shapes, are arranged in groups of threes, with gold grape leaves hiding the divisions between the sections. *(Private collection).*

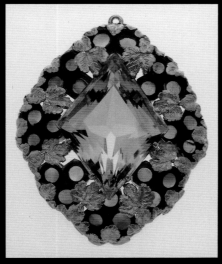

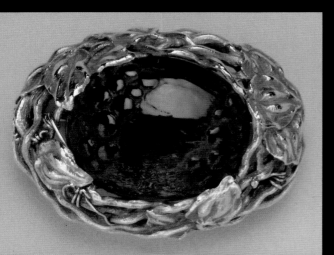

68. Tiffany exploited the grape motif to the full. Instead of faceting the front of this amethyst, he carved grapes into the stone while faceting the back to allow light to reflect the decorated side. *(Collection of Ira Simon).*

69. On this pendant brooch, two black opals are surrounded by enameled grape motifs. Tiffany selected particular black opals whose coloration resembled peacock feathers. *(Collection of Gladys and Robert Koch).*

70. Tiffany used sapphires and demantoid garnets to accent the blue and green shades in black opals. On this pendant, grape vines with leaves and berries encircle the black opal, and the motif continues on the jump ring. *(Collection of Ira Simon).*

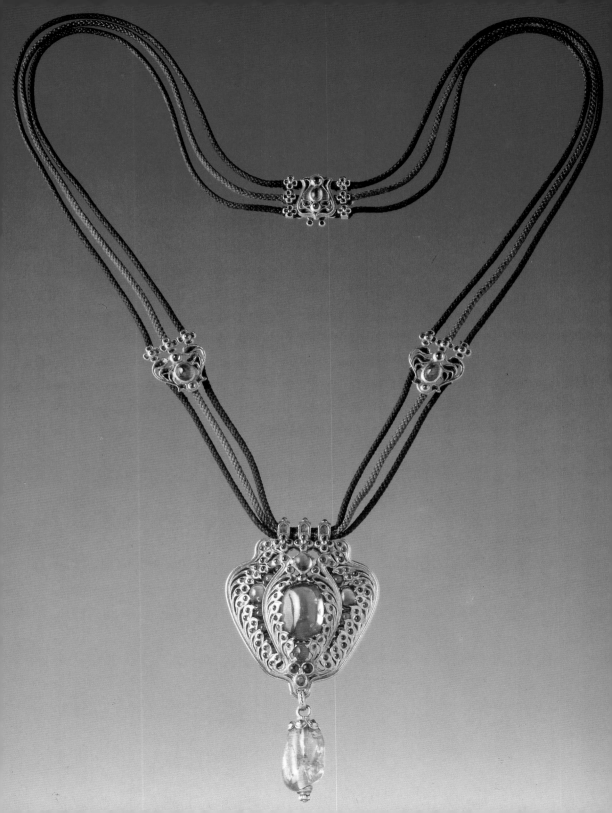

71. Inspired by examples of Indian jewelry, Tiffany designed this piece based on necklaces worn by Hindu men. Blues and greens are evident in the choice of sapphires and emeralds, as well as in the enameling and silk cords. *(Private collection).*

72. This page from Meta Overbeck's sketchbook includes a sketch of a necklace with silk cords, similar to the one opposite. *(Charles Hosmer Morse Museum of American Art, Winter Park, FL).*

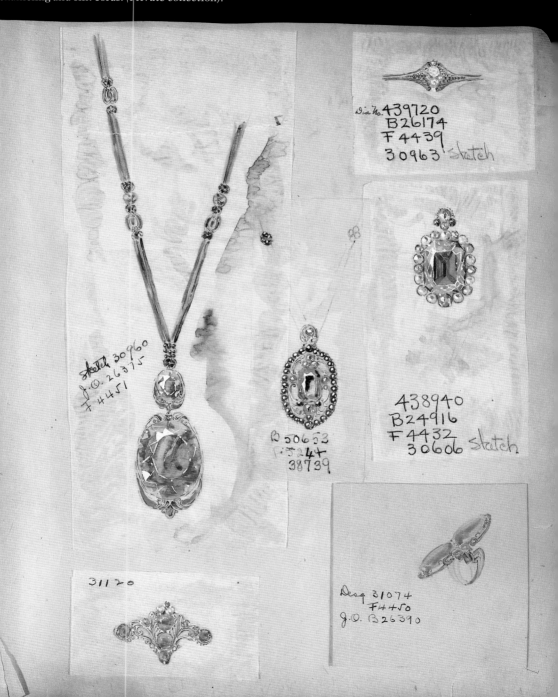

Lapis lazuli with its true deep navy color fascinated Tiffany, who often contrasted it with green stones or enameling. A single jade bead acts as a counterpoint to the blue lapis on a necklace; the center bead and two others are decorated with gold filigree work. Oval and square lapis buttons are set in plaques

58   of black and green enameling on a bracelet. Instead of just polishing these stones, Tiffany decided to engrave them with fluting, an Eastern influence dating from the early Indo-Hellenistic period when beads were cut into spherical, barrel, cylindrical, and disk shapes.

On another bracelet, the center section is set with a large oval lapis, surrounded by four smaller stones and gold filigree work that is Byzantine inspired. A necklace in the jewelry drawing scrapbook, numbered F5165, is similar to this bracelet and would date to *c.* 1920. The spiral motif can be seen on

54   another bracelet where the filigree is similar to decorations in Celtic interlocking designs and brooches found in the Saxon graves of Kent.[29]

The underside of this bracelet was finished with the same attention to detail as the front; it was clearly meant to be admired on both sides. The back of a jewel is the real test of a craftsman's skill. A good jeweler finishes the back with the same meticulous care as the front, whereas a mediocre jeweler uses it to cover his mistakes. When a Louis Tiffany jewel is turned over, the beauty of his design is readily apparent.

Translucent gemstones allow light to pass through but diffuse it so that objects on the other side are not clearly visible. Moonstones, like glass that Tiffany used on his candlesticks in the chapel in the 1893 World's Columbian Exposition in Chicago and on the balustrade and fireplace screen in the Havemeyer mansion, have this almost see-through quality, and may have reminded him of his earlier glass vases as well as the diffused light evident in the sky of his early paintings, executed while he was in Africa. The bluish iridescent moonstones were readily available at the turn of the century, imported from

46   southern Sri Lanka, and were used frequently by Tiffany. In one necklace, a pendant moonstone is suspended from a gold mounting with subdued enameled blue tones that are continued in the stylized leaves and in the Montana sapphires. This piece is a unique example of Tiffany's jewelry, since it bears little similarity to his objects deriving from either naturalistic or historic sources. Rather, it resembles the work of Arts and Crafts designers in Boston at the time. It is numbered J2712 and was designed under the directorship of Julia Munson in *c.* 1912–13. The chain on this necklace is a variation of a trace chain in which the links are joined together alternately in horizontal and vertical planes. Tiffany used this type of chain on his earlier jewelry, during Munson's tenure. He may have seen an illustration of a similar chain in an article by J. L. Bertrand, ''Le Bijou en 1904'' in *Revue de la bijouterie, joaillerie, orfèvrerie.*[30] It was also extensively

73. On this opulent necklace, Tiffany combined sapphires, emeralds and yellow diamonds with yellow and green enamel. The center stone in the pendant is a blue sapphire of 37.49 carats. It was evidently made around 1920.

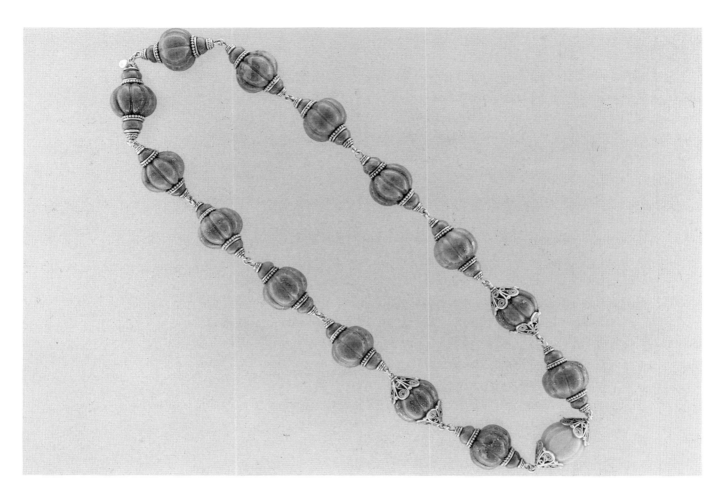

The interesting feature in this gold necklace is that the lapis and jade beads have been fluted. Alternating beads are decorated with filigree work.

used at the turn of the century by designers in the Wiener Werkstätte as well as French Art Nouveau jewelers, especially Lucien Gautrait.

Opals are translucent and have a milky iridescence. When light penetrates the opal in a brooch, the intricate filigree work underneath can be 61 seen, although in a diffused manner. In the case of one pendant necklace, the underside clearly shows how Tiffany bridged the cut-out gold work over the back of the stone so that the image of the gold work would be visible when the light shone through.

Black opals and boulder opals intrigued Tiffany. Their dense and almost mysterious qualities seem to mesmerize the viewer. Black opals are blended with complementary colors of blue enameling and demantoid garnets. In all his opal jewelry, the stone takes precedence over the mounting. Rings are set with a large stone, the gold shank made up of intertwining leaves and branches, while necklaces contain oval stones suspended within gold mounts with coordinating enamel and stones. Two large black opals in one of his brooches are 69 encircled by enameled vines and leaves that hug and overlap the stones, almost embracing them to ensure that they do not fall from their mounting. The blues and greens in these stones appear as if they have been painted with brush strokes in the guise of peacock feathers. The peacock as an image was used extensively during the latter part of the 19th century and early part of the 20th in both the Arts and Crafts and Art Nouveau movements. Tiffany used it in many areas of his oeuvre. Here, instead of depicting the actual bird, he suggests the sheen of the feathers in the color tones of the stones. This brooch is similar to number F3901, illustrated in the photographic album, and would date to *c.* 1918.

64   Boulder opals were rarely used in jewelry design. The opal in one of Tiffany's brooches was left in its iron-stained matrix, giving the appearance of an eye. Tiffany often took advantage of forms in their natural state, in this instance extracting the opal along with the crack in which it was formed. He totally surrounded the stone with elongated leaves, similar to tobacco leaves, using round stylized flowers with yellow beryls to counterbalance the linearity of the leaves.

Louis Comfort Tiffany was an artist, interior decorator and designer of decorative art objects, but he had little or no training as a gemologist. Although his father owned a prestigious jewel house and he had access to some of the choicest gems in the world, his selection of stones was not the precious gemstones Tiffany & Co. featured in their jewelry. Opals, lapis, jade,

The underside of a piece of Louis Comfort Tiffany jewelry is finished with the same attention to detail as the front. On the last section of the bracelet and on the section above the necklace pendant, below left, the mark "Tiffany & Co." is clearly visible. *(Collection of Gladys and Robert Koch).*

In the necklace, below right, a platinum-mounted moonstone is suspended from a pierced gold mounting, enameled and set with Montana sapphires. The design of this necklace bears a resemblance to pieces made in the Arts and Crafts style in England and Boston. *(Collection of Leah Gordon).*

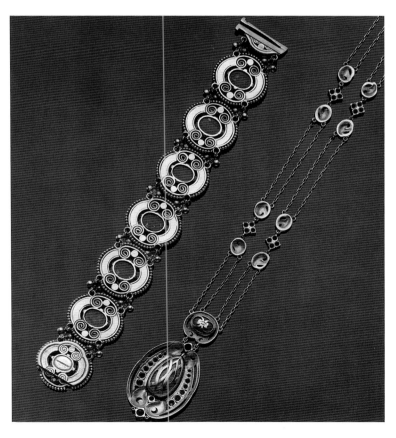

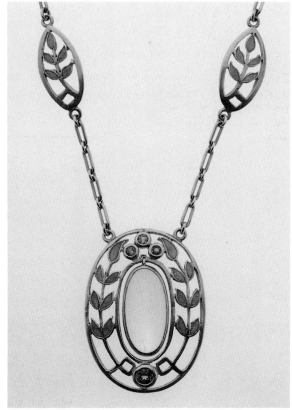

moonstones, and other stones commonly used in jewelry created by the Art Nouveau and Arts and Crafts designers, were not part of the repertoire that Tiffany & Co. considered suitable for their clientele. Louis Tiffany had extensive experience in design and had conducted many experiments in glass at his Corona Glass Works but there is no recorded source to verify that he was cognizant of the different properties of gemstones. My own guess is that the gemstones he incorporated in his jewelry were individually selected by George Frederick Kunz, Tiffany & Co.'s gem expert.

Kunz, who joined Tiffany & Co. on 1 September 1879 at the age of 23, traveled the world in search of unusual gems and gem materials and wrote prolifically of his findings. He collaborated for many years with Paulding Farnham, art director of Tiffany & Co., selecting appropriate gem materials for jewelry and silverware exhibited at international expositions from 1889 to 1904. Kunz assembled two collections of gems, minerals, and ornamental stones, displayed in the 1889 and 1900 Expositions Universelles in Paris, both of which were later purchased by J. Pierpont Morgan for the American Museum of Natural History.

Although no information exists as to the exact working relationship between Louis Tiffany and Kunz, other than the fact that they served together on the Board of Directors of Tiffany & Co., it becomes increasingly apparent when examining the materials Tiffany used in his jewelry that in all likelihood he relied upon Kunz's expertise to choose appropriate materials. One example is the use of turquoise, which both Louis Tiffany and Tiffany & Co. incorporated into their jewelry. For the 1900 Exposition Universelle in Paris, Paulding Farnham contributed a diamond and turquoise tiara[31] in which the stones are perfect, unlike the spider web turquoise in Louis Tiffany's necklace. One can speculate that Kunz was collecting gemstones and materials for both Tiffany & Co. and Louis Tiffany jewelry, emphasizing quality and value for one and color and uniqueness for the other.

Kunz's extensive travels included the Americas, and it was probably he who brought back a selection of quartz arrowheads that Tiffany included as pendants in several necklaces in 1912. Kunz was also aware of the various properties of pure gold, which is normally considered too soft for utilitarian purposes. Pure gold scratches and bends very easily and is rarely used for personal adornment. Kunz would have known how it could be worked to advantage, as can be seen in the elaborate Adams Vase, now in the Metropolitan Museum of Art, on which he collaborated with Paulding Farnham in 1893. The body of the vase was made of pure gold, mined in Forest City, California. Similarly, Kunz may have suggested to Louis Tiffany that he experiment with hammering pellets or "shots" of gold to create two organic pendant sections on a necklace. The lower portion was worked into the shape of a maple seed, characteristic of Tiffany's love of plants.

Kunz was associated with Tiffany & Co. until his death in 1932, a year before Louis Tiffany died and his jewelry and enameling department was closed. In all likelihood, he conferred with Tiffany about gemstones and worked with Julia Munson and Meta Overbeck on a more detailed level, as needed. He may have shown the stones for approval to Tiffany, who would then hand them over to his designers with specific instructions for creating a particular type of jewel.

Initially, Tiffany had to approve every piece created in his department. I believe that, as the years passed and he became involved in such projects as the Tiffany Foundation, he relied more and more on Overbeck and her judgment for detailed designs of a piece of jewelry. No information exists about her background training, where she worked before coming to Tiffany's jewelry and enameling department, or what happened to her after she left. Those jewelry pieces which can be attributed to her are stronger and bolder in conception and execution than those designed by Munson. Materials such as carved jade and coral, which are normally associated with the Art Deco period, are illustrated both in her jewelry drawing and in the photographic scrapbooks. Numbers F4029, 4131, and 4186 in the photographic album contain carved pieces of jadeite, a material that one would not normally associate with Louis Tiffany. An illustration on page 15 in the jewelry drawing scrapbook depicts a drop earring in carved jadeite, number F5291, which would date to *c.* 1922, while the earlier examples date to *c.* 1918. In this case, according to the notation on the drawing, an earring was made to accommodate a ''customer's ear drop''. Another jadeite pendant, on page 29 in the sketchbook, is numbered F5670 (*c.* 1925), while a necklace on page 33, number F5713, would date to *c.* 1926. Tiffany continued to produce this type of jewelry for many years.

The drawing scrapbook also contains several pages of geometrically conceived designs. One bracelet on page 25 is constructed with truncated triangular plaques attached onto the main body of the bracelet, much like a crenelated molding. Another, on page 23, has a central square section set with a pink stone, with enamel demarcating the attached stepped motif on each side, and continued in the rectangular links on the bracelet itself. These bracelets are numbered F5461 and 5430 and would date to *c.* 1923.

Another drawing on page 22 is similar to a lapis and enamel brooch. This is number F5490 and would date to *c.* 1923, a late date when one considers the Art Deco examples above. Although Tiffany did make a few revolutionary pieces in the new style, most of his jewelry still reflected his interest in nature.

Tiffany's brooches with the intricate vine and leaf motif were executed under Meta Overbeck and date from 1915 to 1925. He often used grape motifs on his amethyst jewelry. On one brooch, a diamond-shaped faceted amethyst, set into a platinum box, was inlaid into a gold mounting. The surrounding mounting was divided into eight sections, each with three amethysts cut into flat hexagonal shapes that fit together like a jigsaw puzzle. Gold grape leaves rim the edge and serve to hide the divisions between the amethyst sections. Like most of Tiffany's jewelry, this piece is three-dimensional and conceived almost along engineering principles.

65

67

Another example of a sculptural piece of jewelry is an amethyst brooch in which the stone was faceted on the back but polished on the front side, then carved with grapes. The motif is continued in the gold grape vine and leaf motif surrounding the stone. When the ancient Greeks wanted to represent Bacchus, the god of wine, they chose the amethyst to symbolize the purple flood of wine. According to a small, hand-written volume located in the Tiffany & Co. archives, which is entitled *Language of Flowers*, vines symbolized intoxication.[32] In this brooch, Tiffany is emphasizing grapes and wine in his visual figuration of the plant, both on the mounting and carved onto the stone.

68

That Tiffany selected stones not for their monetary value but for their visual appeal held true even in those rare instances when he incorporated precious gemstones into his designs. These were created while Meta Overbeck was director of the department and again gemstones dominate the individual piece of jewelry but color and its effect on the overall design remains dominant.

A necklace which was bought at Tiffany & Co. in 1915 as a wedding present for Ellen DuPont Wheelwright of "Goodstay", Wilmington, Delaware, by her husband, is made up of blue zircons and canary diamonds.[33] In the center of the pendant is a 37 karat blue zircon, surrounded by canary diamonds and zircons with amethysts, demantoid garnets and smaller diamonds of various hues. It hangs from a triple chain of platinum links and pearls. The stones dominate the necklace, again in a coloristic manner.

42

In another instance, a pendant necklace is set with a blue sapphire of 37.49 karats, while emeralds, blue sapphires and yellow diamonds are interspersed with yellow and green enamel. The central stone hangs free from the surrounding mounting. It is conceived in a manner similar to a necklace, F5197, illustrated on page 15 in the jewelry drawing scrapbook and would date to *c.* 1920. The central sapphire has been replaced with several smaller stones. These pendant necklaces continued to be offered while the department was open, even after the style was no longer popular.

73

Perhaps the most spectacular piece designed by Tiffany is the necklace inspired by Indian examples, number F3332, dating to *c.* 1918, with a

71

Tiffany continued the grape motif onto the underside of the black opal pendant necklace in Ill. 70. *(Collection of Ira Simon).*

Opposite, a page from Meta Overbeck's scrapbook showing a variety of her jewelry designs. *(Charles Hosmer Morse Museum of American Art, Winter Park, FL).*

Size 4½

B 51780 Order
F 5296 6 ...
39353 8 ...

Sketch 39666
B 5275 ×
F 5319.

Order - F 5285
Order - B 51675
Sketch - 39068.

Size 6

Des. 39652
Order B 52708
Sketch H. F 5316

J.O. B 51614
Ord. F 5286
Sketch 38707

B. 52792
F 5325

Size 6½

B 55868
40791
F 5404

18"

Changed to small
ball chain.

B 56986
F 5379
40532

B 52900

F 5329

Sketch 38917
F 5197
B 50969

26
chain.

Sketch to put
locks adds
to cut
out go

Sketch H. F 5290
Order. B 51736
Sketch 39264
Size 5½

F 5339

B 54536

F 5291
B 51680
480027

38772

Sk. 39613
B 52721
F 5315

See photo of F 5126
Page 256
9 large stones changed
for emeralds.

sapphire set into the pendant and an emerald drop, although it is not a superb stone. Rubies, sapphires, and emeralds en cabochon are placed within gold feather-like motifs to complement the central stone. In place of link chains, Tiffany used silk cords in complementary green and blue colors, similar to a pendant necklace on the first page in the jewelry drawing scrapbook, number F4451, which would date it to *c*. 1920. The slides that have been enameled and set with gemstones decorate the cords. Among the jewelry listed in the Laurelton Hall inventory are two "Hindoo" necklaces, both strung on silk cord bands.[34] These are reminiscent of Mughal jewelry with its polychrome enameling, use of green, blue and red colorations, and unfaceted polished stones, and are similar to two examples illustrated by Thomas Holbein Hendley in *The Journal of Indian Art*, plate 32, No. 219, and plate 46, No. 316.[35] Both pendants are suspended from flat plaited chains in place of traditional silk cords. This type of necklace was worn only by men, chiefly Brahmins or Hindu merchants. In the first decade of the 20th century, there was a renewed interest in Indian jewelry brought about by the two visits of durbars to the coronations in 1902 and 1910 in London. The elaborate displays of their caparisoned elephants and jeweled princes were recorded in the newspapers and served as a source of inspiration. Tiffany may also have been influenced by the collection of Indian jewelry that his former partner, Lockwood de Forest, assembled for the Metropolitan Museum of Art in 1915. Although the illustrated examples in the Museum's *Bulletin*[36] for that year do not include a necklace similar in style to the above example, Tiffany may have used objects from this collection for inspiration.

A great variety of jewelry was produced during the 26 years that Louis Tiffany's enameling and jewelry division was in operation at Tiffany & Co. I estimate that approximately 5,500 pieces were created during this period, *i.e.*, approximately four to five pieces each week. This may not seem like a substantial output in terms of mass production in the commercial sense; however, when considering that each piece was a one-of-a-kind item and hand-made, the magnitude of his work in jewelry is impressive indeed! Louis Tiffany was unquestionably the driving force behind this remarkable output. It is equally certain that his capable principal designers, Julia Munson and Meta Overbeck, imparted their distinctive styles to the jewelry they not only designed but also produced.

5

The Final Years:
The Jeweled Splendors

As a creative artist, Louis Comfort Tiffany was continually searching for new challenges. In his relentless pursuit of beauty, he never rested on his laurels; instead he looked toward fresh fields for his creativity, and disdained the notion of repeating his previous artistic achievements. After succeeding in one area, he would turn to another, stretching beyond his prior accomplishments.

Enameling on copper had proved an extremely successful endeavor, and Tiffany was proud of what he had accomplished. Samuel Howe related an instance when Tiffany compared one of his enameled vases against precious and semi-precious gemstones at Tiffany & Co. to "measure the tone in the color." He concluded that his enamels "proved equally fine in quality and tone of color with the gems . . . especially the blues and the intense greens, showed much more depth and perspective than were found in the stones."[1]

At Tiffany Furnaces, Tiffany's enamelware had all been made of copper. But once that firm was incorporated into Tiffany & Co., he was offered the opportunity to use precious metals as a base material and gemstones to complement the enamel decoration. Not surprisingly, Tiffany produced few copper pieces after 1907. Instead, he chose to exploit the wide aesthetic possibilities of gold and silver, metals that Tiffany & Co. was particularly well equipped to shape in both traditional and novel ways. At the same time, his work in gold and silver holloware was not a separate entity of his oeuvre but a natural progression from his enamels on copper and his jewelry, both of which had been favorably received on the international scene. In particular, shapes previously derived from flowers and plants now became formalized, based on traditional forms and medieval ecclesiastical ware.

Tiffany's exploration into silver and gold holloware has been largely overlooked. I believe this is the result of confusion generated by the marks on the underside of these objects. Although all these pieces were designed by Louis Tiffany, they were made at Tiffany & Co., and consequently bear Tiffany & Co. marks. Normally, the mark is made up of the following four lines:

Tiffany & Co.
Pattern number/MAKERS/Order number
Precious metal content
President's initial.

The first line is self-explanatory. The second includes the pattern number, assigned to each particular form and used on all pieces in that form, regardless of decoration. These numbers run consecutively, beginning with 1, dating to the 1850s. Thus, all Tiffany holloware can be roughly dated on the basis of these pattern numbers.[2] MAKERS indicates that the piece was made at the Tiffany & Co. workshop which was located, at the time Louis Tiffany's objects were produced, in Forest Hills, New Jersey (a section of Newark). The number appearing after MAKERS is an order number assigned to every holloware request.

The third line is stamped with the metal content, which in the case of sterling silver was either spelled out or stamped 925–1000 (indicating 925 parts of silver out of 1,000). For items made with gold, GOLD and the karat weight were stamped.[3]

The fourth line consists of the current Tiffany & Co. president's initial. ''C'' indicates the period from 1902 to 1907, when Charles Cook was president. Upon his death in 1907, John C. Moore, the son of Edward C. Moore, took over the reins of the company until 1947. This period is designated by a script ''M.'' Some pieces bear an abbreviated mark, Tiffany & Co./Metal Content/ President's initial, which means they were made in Tiffany's enameling and jewelry workshop in New York. Holloware forms were spun in the New Jersey facility and then sent to the New York store for finishing, including enameling and gem setting.

Tiffany used plique-à-jour enameling on simple silver vessels. The detail below of a bonbon dish made in 1913 shows the areas that have been pierced out of the metal and filled with green, red, yellow and mauve enameling. *(Collection of the author)*.

Below right, this piece of holloware (the underside of Ill. 78) shows all the Tiffany & Co. marks, giving pattern number, makers, metal content, etc. *(Allentown Art Museum, Gift of Bethlehem Steel Corp., 1985)*.

The Louis Tiffany items produced in the Tiffany & Co. workshops were made, like his jewelry, under the direction of Julia Munson and Dr. Parker McIlhinney. McIlhinney was placed on the payroll on 1 November 1909, and shared his duties between the sixth floor of the New York store and Tiffany's silver division in Forest Hills. According to an employee ledger in the Tiffany & Co. archives, one-third of McIlhinney's salary of $4,400 per annum was charged to the sixth-floor jewelry department while the additional amount was billed to Forest Hills. He remained in the newly formed department until 1 August 1914,[4] continuing to create the necessary chemicals for Tiffany's enamelware on precious metals as he had done previously at Tiffany Furnaces.

A 6 July 1906 listing under "Silver Shop-Forest Hills" in a Tiffany & Co. employee ledger records a silver designer, Albert A. Southwick, "working under direction of Mr. Louis C. Tiffany."[5] His most notable creation had been an elaborate 119-piece service for the battleship *New Jersey*, made in 1906. Before coming to Tiffany's, he had been schooled in art in Europe, studying steel-engraving at the Craftsman School in Berlin and, in 1898, at the Ecole des Beaux Arts in Paris.[6] With his artistic training, experience and expertise in creating silver, he would have been a natural choice to supervise the making of Louis Tiffany's holloware, especially until McIlhinney was transferred to the new department.

Louis Tiffany's precious metal holloware objects were a collaboration between the silversmiths, directed by either Southwick or McIlhinney, and the sixth-floor jewelry shop. Although this represented a new departure for Louis Tiffany, it was not his first involvement with silver. Several years before, he had been adorning his favrile glass vessels with precious metal mountings. The first evidence of this dates to around 1897 when, under the direction of Siegfried Bing, Edward Colonna designed silver-gilt mountings to embellish Tiffany's favrile glass vessels.[7] Within a few years, Tiffany was collaborating with Paulding Farnham at Tiffany & Co. on similar designs. As a result, they jointly contributed eight examples of their work to the Tiffany & Co. display at the 1900 Exposition Universelle in Paris, Tiffany providing the favrile glass vessels, and Farnham designing the gold and gem-set mounts.[8]

The Tiffany & Co. archives includes a folder, marked "Tiffany Glass", that contains numerous drawings of vessels made up of favrile glass with silver mountings. Although none of these drawings is signed (very few in the archives are), we can assume that they were Louis Tiffany's designs, since the vessels are made of favrile glass and the mounts are designed in a much more organic manner than would normally have been the case for Tiffany & Co. pieces. I have first-hand knowledge of only two pieces based on these drawings; both are inkwells dating to about 1900, one in the Newark Museum and the other in the

Charles Hosmer Morse Museum of American Art.[9] The number engraved into the glass on each of these objects is prefixed by an "o" which, according to Martin Eidelberg, indicates that they were made before the turn of the century.[10]

In 1907, Tiffany & Co. advertised "Tiffany Favrile Carved Glass . . . A new Favrile Glass product made under the supervision of Mr. Louis C. Tiffany . . . Clear crystal with hand-carved decoration, also with hand-carved colored decorations . . . with relief and intaglio decorations. Each piece bears the marks 'L.C. Tiffany-Favrile'." The following items were listed with silver mountings: claret jugs, cologne bottles, inkstands, rose jars and vases.[11] Like the earlier examples that Tiffany designed with Colonna and Farnham, these pieces were a combination of Tiffany's glass with precious metal mounts, and were probably produced from 1906 when Southwick began to work under Louis Tiffany's direction. The notation in the *Blue Book* indicates that this was a "new Favrile Glass product." In fact, a listing in a Tiffany & Co. ledger for October 1906 lists eleven items as "Tiffany Glass-Silver" in pattern numbers from 16799 to 16809, including vases, inkstands, ring stands and a pin tray.[12] One example, which may be considered part of this group although it dates to 1909, is a cameo bowl in the Chrysler Museum.[13] Cameo oak leaves that have green centers and borders decorate the clear glass; the motif continues onto the scalloped sterling silver rim. This piece is conceived as a salad or fruit bowl in a traditional form. It lacks the fluid organic feeling one normally associates with Tiffany's creations but could be considered a precursor to his more important carved glass vessels with enameled and gem-set mounts.

It is not known what working relationship Louis Tiffany maintained with Tiffany & Co. for the manufacture of silver mounts for his favrile glass vessels. He probably sent the glass vessels to Tiffany & Co. with instructions to make the appropriate mounts which, although decorated with repoussé or etching, were neither enameled nor set with gemstones. They continued to be advertised in the company's catalogues until 1910.

After the 3 May 1907 business agreement between Louis Tiffany and Tiffany & Co., a selection of his carved glass vessels became embellished with enameling and gemstones. One example, a carved cameo glass inkwell, is 74 listed under the heading "Tiffany Enamels" in the 1909 *Blue Book* as "inkstands of richly carved glass, enameled cover set with opals."[14] The silver mounting is set with carnelians and fire opals, their orange colors contrasting with the green pearl-like lumps as well as champlevé enameling surrounding each gem. The central stone, a polished fire opal, was chosen for its unusual interior formation, resembling rocky outcroppings of the Grand Canyon. The mounting is signed "Tiffany & Co. Makers Sterling Silver C". Although the "C" normally indicates that the object was made between 1902 and 1907, during Charles Cook's presidency, these initial designations were often not changed for several months after the death of the president.[15] This inkwell appears to have been made just after the department transferred in May 1907. It may have been in the process of manufacture at that date and, when the enameling division was absorbed into Tiffany & Co., the gemstones and enameling were added.

Along with the silver-mounted cameo glass that Louis Tiffany created, he also designed holloware items after the move to Tiffany & Co. These were all one-of-a-kind pieces and relate to the "objets de vertu" that Fabergé was designing in Russia, J. Tostrup in Norway, and Feuillâtre in France. For the most part, they were small objects, similar to the enamel on copper vessels that Tiffany produced in the EL series either at Stourbridge Glass Co. or, after 1902, at Tiffany Furnaces. They were made of sterling silver, 18 or 22 karat gold and, less frequently, copper; they were enameled either in translucent colors or with plique-à-jour, their surfaces often enhanced with gemstones.

Although Tiffany was not a metallurgist, his advisers would have been aware of the properties of gold and silver and the correct standards for successful results. Alexander Fisher cautions, "It is better to use silver a little above the standard, as it is more flexible; and gold ought not to be less than 18 carats."[16]

One of the photographic scrapbooks in the Tiffany & Co. archives includes several pages of small vases, covered boxes, powder boxes, and trays, each assigned a three-digit number preceded by the letter "J", indicating, as we have seen, that the object was made under the directorship of Julia Munson. There are approximately 25 examples in this scrapbook with numbers from 270 to 720, interspersed with similarly marked jewelry items.

All of Tiffany's early precious metal holloware pieces were enameled and often set with the following gemstones: opals, turquoise, malachite, pearls, jade, or garnets. Two small gold bowls, J371 and J433, were created in much the same manner as the small bowls in the EL 80–90 series, their surfaces enameled with flowers and leaves and set with either garnets or opals. There were several small silver covered boxes, similar to examples in the SG 180–190 series but without knobs, numbered J715, 716, 719 and 720. There were four vases, three enameled with plant motifs and the fourth, J674, with a geometric pattern. J430, a long-necked vase, was decorated in repoussé with a pitcher plant. To enhance its importance, it was mounted on a wooden pedestal as Chinese vases were. The form of J432 tapers from a wide shoulder until three-quarters to the base, which flares out slightly. J556 is a small bulbous vase decorated with Japanese Paulownia leaves. J428 is the only enameled box within this group that was made of copper. Like the boxes in the SG 180–190 series, it has a knob for grasping.

The gold dandelion vase which is the first known piece of holloware executed at Tiffany & Co. after the 1907 consolidation of Louis Tiffany's jewelry and enamel department. *(Private collection)*.

The only extant piece from this series, a small gold vase (J421), was champlevé enameled with dandelions, a decoration reminiscent of the lamp that Louis Tiffany exhibited in the 1900 Paris Exposition Universelle and the 1901 Buffalo Pan-American Exposition. Rather than decorating the surface with puff balls as had done on his earlier lamps, the plant is depicted in its flowering stage, complete with luscious green leaves and vivid yellow flowers. These are executed in a manner similar to a nature sketch signed by A. C. Gouvy, which may have been the source for the vase.

The vase is stamped "Tiffany & Co./MAKERS/Gold" with the initial "C", which would indicate that it was made during Charles Cook's tenure, *i.e.*, between 1902 to 1907. However, since Tiffany & Co. was not in the business of producing Louis Tiffany's enamelware until after 3 May 1907, this piece, like the carved cameo inkwell mentioned earlier, may have been made just after the department was established. Since this piece relates to the dandelion drawing which is stamped "Tiffany Furnaces," perhaps Tiffany had designed it earlier, intending for it to be created in copper at Tiffany Furnaces. After the department was moved, he may have decided to make it out of gold, now plentiful at the Tiffany & Co. workshops.

These gold and silver holloware items were advertised in Tiffany & Co.'s *Blue Books* from 1909 through 1914. The 1911 edition listed a sampling of such articles under "Tiffany Enamel" as "fancy cabinet pieces . . . match boxes of silver and enamel and powder boxes of silver and gold overlay, enameled and set with precious and semi-precious stones, vases."[17] They ranged in price from $10 for small items to $900 for more elaborate vases.

Although the exact date is not known, within a few years after establishing a jewelry and enameling division at Tiffany & Co., Louis Tiffany began to create precious metal objects with plique-à-jour enameling. Plique-à-jour is constructed with cells, similar to cloisonné, filled with transparent enamel in powder form. This technique can be accomplished in one of two ways. Normally, a copper foil is applied to the reverse side of the metal, serving as a backing for the enamel, and subsequently peeled off after firing. If the pierced area is less than $\frac{1}{16}$ of an inch, no backing is needed. Instead, enamel is mixed with gum of tragacanth to make a paste that is packed into the spaces. Capillary forces in the mixture hold the enamel in place during firing.[18] Without a metal backing on one side of the enamel, light can penetrate, creating an effect similar to that of stained glass.

This technique was popular at the turn of the century when J. Tostrup displayed several elaborate floral-inspired chalices with plique-à-jour enameling at the 1900 Exposition Universelle in Paris.[19] Louis Tiffany also exhibited at this exposition and may have seen these pieces. There were similar exhibits at the Paris Salon of 1902 by Eugène Feuillâtre and André Fernand Thesmar, and at the Salon of 1903 by Raoul Wagner, a less well-known French jeweler.[20]

The next known piece of holloware designed by Louis Comfort Tiffany is a 22 karat gold trumpet-shaped vase decorated with alternating panels of champlevé and plique-à-jour enameling in the form of Gothic lancet windows. Geometric shapes of squares and circles decorated with spirals and rosettes are enameled in green, blue, yellow and rose. A notation in the Tiffany & Co. ledgers cites 4 October 1911 as the completion date for this piece. Later, Tiffany produced many silver and gold holloware pieces with plique-à-jour, often in simple, usable vessels such as a bonbon dish made in 1913. The enameled colors of green, red, blue, yellow, and mauve which pierce the sides of the dish are visible only when light is reflected from underneath.

It is not known how many precious metal holloware pieces Louis Tiffany designed; however, the years 1912 to 1916 seem to have been his most productive ones, even though he continued to make selected items after 1916. Listed in a Tiffany & Co. ledger are the following five enameled objects: a box with enameled panels, 18454; an enameled inkwell, 18469; a box with goldfish and enameled cover, 18476; an inkwell with enameled panels, 18477; and a photo frame with enameled panels, 18478. The enameled areas on the four objects, 18454 and those with consecutive numbers from 18476 to 18478, are painted not directly onto the vessel but onto panels which are attached to the body of the holloware. It is much easier to enamel a flat surface, which can then be applied to a vertical or horizontal surface. These objects are not treated like Tiffany's earlier repoussé enamels on copper where colors were allowed to blend with one another; rather, enameled areas are carefully demarcated either through champlevé or cloisonné enameling or, as in the above examples, on separate panels that are attached to a holloware form. The enameled areas are treated in a much more formalized manner, not typical of Tiffany's earlier work.

Pattern 18477 is a hexagonal inkwell with enameled panels in a   75
floral design that seems to resemble Queen Anne's lace. It is traditional in form
but the stiffness of the shape is softened by an interesting play of greens, oranges,
and maroons in the enameled areas, more in keeping with Tiffany's earlier
enamels on copper. This inkwell has an interesting history, having been bought
by George E. Booth for the Detroit Institute of Arts in 1920.[21] Booth was a
prominent Detroit newspaper publisher and patron of the arts, who founded the
Cranbrook Academy of Art.

Tiffany created two silver boxes with enameled panels: number
18454 completed on 14 November 1913, and 18476, completed on 31 October of
the same year.[22] The latter is a small circular box with slightly domed cover and a
copper panel set into the lid. There is a notation on the drawing for this box,
"enameled top sent under separate cover," indicating that the box was made in
the New Jersey facility while the lid was enameled on the sixth-floor jewelry shop
in New York. The enameled panel depicts in an impressionistic manner a fish of
goldfish coloring, swimming amid seaweed. The fish's body is arranged in a
similar manner to fish on an opalescent glass window, illustrated in *Der Moderne
Stil* in 1902.[23]

Perhaps the most spectacular precious metal object that Louis
Tiffany created is the 18-karat gold jewel box (18397), based on his "Four   82
Seasons" window. Tiffany exhibited this window in the following three
expositions at the turn of the century: the 1900 Exposition Universelle in Paris,
the 1901 Pan-American Exposition in Buffalo, and the 1902 Esposizione d'Arte
Decorativa Moderna in Turin. The window was later taken apart and installed in
Tiffany's living room at Laurelton Hall. The jewel box closely follows the design
of the window. Without knowledge of the box, Herwin Schaefer wrote the
following analysis of the window which, upon close examination, also describes
the box: "a composition of four cartouche-shaped scenes of the seasons, banded
by pearl and guilloche, the whole framed by a border of leafy scrolls growing from
five vases in the lower part . . . The center space between the four season panels is
filled with frothy bubble-like shapes."[24] Scenes of the seasons are replicated in
four separate cloisonné enameled panels: tulips beneath a flowering cherry
branch for spring; poppies below a chestnut bough with a meadow and lake
beyond for summer; field corn, grapes, squash and peaches for autumn; and pine
boughs laden with snow above a bonfire for winter. The center bubble-like
mosaics are replaced with gemstones and the five images of amphorae at the
bottom are extended to all four sides of the box.

74. An enameled carved cameo
inkwell designed by Louis Comfort
Tiffany sometime in 1907 is set
with carnelians, and the lid is
crowned by a polished fire opal. The
surface of the stone acts like a piece
of glass that allows the viewer to see
into the crevices of the stone.
*(Collection of Lynne and Michael
Lerner)*.

75. This silver inkstand, decorated with enameled flowers similar to Queen Anne's lace, was made in 1914. It was bought by George E. Booth, a supporter of the American Arts and Crafts movement who founded the Cranbrook Academy of Art. *(The Detroit Institute of Arts, Gift of Mr. George E. Booth).*

76. A 22-karat gold vase made in 1911, decorated with champlevé and plique-à-jour enameling in the shape of Gothic lancet windows in subtle shades of blue, green and yellow. *(Lillian Nassau, Ltd.).*

77-79. The decoration around the upper part of this covered urn, measuring 22 inches high, was based on a painting by Tiffany, of around 1898, called "Spring" (far right). *(Charles Hosmer Morse Museum of American Art, Winter Park, FL)*. The urn, which was shown at the 1915 Panama-Pacific Exposition in San Francisco, depicts on one side a procession of young maidens paying homage to Flora, and on the other Ceres riding in her carriage with maidens carrying baskets of fruit to denote a bountiful harvest. *(The Allentown Museum of Art, Gift of Bethlehem Steel Corp., 1985)*.

80. This tulip-shaped plique-à-jour gold chalice (right), decorated with peacock feathers, was made in 1925 and is the last known piece of holloware that Tiffany designed. *(Private collection)*.

81. A gold cup (far right) with plique-à-jour enameling in shades of blue and turquoise in an Indian pattern. It was finished on 13 July 1913 and exhibited at the Panama-Pacific Exposition in San Francisco, where Henry Walters bought it. *(Walters Art Gallery, Baltimore, MD)*.

82. In 1914, Tiffany reproduced his "Four Seasons" stained glass window on the cover of this 18-karat gold jewel box. Scenes of the seasons are shown in four cloisonné panels in the same order as when the window was shown at international exhibitions. The center bubble-like mosaic in the window has been replaced by an assemblage of opals, tourmalines, sapphires and chrysoprases. *(Charles Hosmer Morse Museum of American Art, Winter Park, FL).*

83. For the 1915 San Francisco exhibition, Tiffany designed a gold tea screen based on the "Parakeets and Goldfish Bowl" stained glass window that had attracted attention at the 1893 exhibition in Chicago. It is set into a boxwood base and includes plique-à-jour, opaque, transparent and translucent enameling. *(Collection of Lee and Ray Grover).*

According to a Tiffany & Co. pattern book, this jewel box was finished on 30 April 1914. The box itself was made in the New Jersey silver plant while the enameling and gem-setting were done in the New York department where it was also assembled. Although Louis Tiffany had used gemstones to complement enameling on his holloware just after Tiffany & Co. began to make these objects, this box surpasses anything that he had done up to this time. His selection of gemstones reflected his unending interest in color as well as his love of jewels, which is evident from his twelve-year involvement in jewelry design. Tourmalines, blue and pink sapphires, and chrysoprases complement colors in the enameled areas. The white translucent color tones in opals, a favorite stone in Tiffany's jewelry, were used to complement the enameled cartouches and the background area. There is no doubt that Tiffany created this box as a reminder of his beloved "Four Seasons" window when all the parts were intact at the exhibitions. Although it is not known whether he retained this jewel box for his own collection, it is certainly a treasure that can be enjoyed both visually and tactilely.

Concurrently with the above items, Tiffany was also creating objects to be exhibited in the 1915 Panama-Pacific Exposition, to be held in San Francisco. Since several of these pieces date as early as 1912, he probably made the objects and, like selected pieces of his enamels on copper, retained his favorites until he showed them in this exhibition. All the objects he displayed in San Francisco were stamped with Tiffany & Co. marks along with an additional special mark, indicating that they were part of this display: "ЧP" (for Panama-Pacific), followed by an identifying number.

At this exhibition, Louis Tiffany's was the only work contributed by Tiffany & Co. His display, listed under "Sculpture", was housed in Gallery 71 in the Palace of Fine Arts, along with the work of American painters such as George Luks.[25] Other prominent painters whose work was included in the pavilion were William Merritt Chase, Childe Hassam, John Singer Sargent, and James Abbott McNeill Whistler.

An article in *The Jewelers' Circular* describes the thirteen objects that he contributed, arranged in three cases: two vases were highlighted in individual cases and the other eleven items were in one long case.

The largest and most elaborate . . . is a hand-wrought silver gilt vase ornamented with jewels and enamel. The center border is set with horns of plenty, carved from pure gold. The fruit pouring from the horns is represented by precious and semi-precious stones. Above the jeweled band are drops of jewels set with green enamel stones and Mexican opals. The body and neck are richly decorated with bands of champlevé enamel. The handles are pierced silver, enameled and set with corals. The feet are carved and enameled to repeat in bolder form the decoration of the handles. Among the stones used in the border are sapphires,

84. Tiffany continued to make vessels out of precious metals after the San Francisco exhibition, such as this plique-à-jour gold chalice. The cup is held by armatures, set with alternating cabochon jade and amethysts that continue onto the stem and the foot. Made in 1916, the chalice was owned by Henry Walters and sold at the sale of Mrs. Walters's art collection in 1943. *(Private collection)*.

rubies, olivines, amethysts, opals, coral, jades, garnets, topaz, tourmalines, rhodelites, chrysophrase [sic], carnelian teryls, turquoise and chalcedony.[26]

The drawing No. 18489 in the Tiffany & Co. archives indicates that the special number for this vase is ¶P14. (As there were only thirteen objects in this exhibition, one wonders if more were planned but not included in the end.) There is a notation in the upper right-hand corner, "drawn from silver," meaning that the drawing was sketched from the piece of silver after it was made. This tour de force of the silversmith's art was 30¾ inches high and was in the shape of a Chinese-type vase, similar to a translucent red glass vase in the collection of the Chrysler Museum.[27] The tapering body does not end in a flat bottom but comes to a point, and the vase is supported by flaring feet. Tiffany retained this vase after the exhibition, displaying it in his retrospective exhibition in 1916 at the Tiffany Studios. (The current whereabouts of this piece is unknown).

The next largest piece, which also occupies a case by itself, is a hand-wrought silver jar with a frieze decoration of transparent enamel. The borders enclosing the panel and decorating the foot and cover of the jar are delicately chased and carved. The frieze is a copy of two mural panels entitled "Flora" and "Ceres," painted by Mr. Tiffany to decorate the dining room of his city residence. The decoration is etched on the vase and then covered with transparent enamel. The particular beauty and rarity of this piece lies in the fact that all the colors, even the flesh tones, are transparent enamel, thus allowing the drawing lines of the etching to give a slight outline to the composition, giving it a totally different appearance from the usual painted enamel decorations.[28]

This vase (18395), which is now in the collection of the Allentown Museum of Art, is smaller than the other, measuring 22 inches in height. The special mark is ¶P13, on the underside of the piece. Unlike Tiffany's previous metalware with enameled decoration, the panels are executed in Limoges enameling. 77,78

A notation on the drawing, "Band of figures scratch etched and enameled from Mr. Tiffany's paintings," confirms the description from *The Jewelers' Circular*. The whereabouts of "Ceres" is unknown. "Flora" is based on a painting commonly called "Spring," which is in the Charles Hosmer Morse Museum of American Art. It is ironic that a statement made by Hugh McKean when speaking of the painting, "The composition has the flow and rhythm of a procession on a classic urn,"[29] applies more aptly to the frieze on the covered jar. The figures on the urn mirror those on the painting with young maidens carrying flowers to Flora, who sits on her throne. Tiffany used his nieces and cousins as models for this painting. According to a descendant, the Flora was Tiffany's niece, Alfreda Mitchell Bingham, who was the daughter of Tiffany's sister, Annie Olivia Tiffany Mitchell. She was the eldest of the cousins and Tiffany adored 79

her.[30] Trees separate the two panels. On the reverse side, Ceres, the Greek goddess of agriculture, rides in her carriage amid maidens carrying baskets of fruit. Once again, Tiffany was inspired by nature, but instead of copying the source directly, he chose to symbolize nature through the personification of ancient goddesses. Both scenes pictorialize nature; one the springtime when flowers are blooming, and the other, the bountiful harvest.

"The other 11 pieces are arranged in a long case. Three of them are small copper vases."[31] Actually, there were only two copper vases.[32] They resemble the small vessels in Tiffany's enamels in the copper EL series. The whereabouts of only one is known today, a vase with its surface enameled in a roughened texture, executed in a similar manner to the branches on a box in the Metropolitan Museum of Art's collection. Also like his previous enameled objects, this bowl is counter enameled and gilt on the underside. Around the shoulder, enameled maple seeds surround groups of opals, either in bunches of two or three. It has been signed with the special exhibition mark ¶P8, and stamped only "Tiffany & Co." without the usual pattern numbers and other markings. This indicates that it was made in the sixth-floor jewelry workshop in New York under the direction of Meta Overbeck.

"A larger piece is a hand-wrought silver cup covered with transparent enamel set in gold cloisonne. The border of peacocks gives the keynote of the decorations, the rich color of the breast being repeated in the lower part of the cup and the sweeping richness of the spread tail repeated in the feet."[33] This cup, No. 18226, is 8½ inches high and was finished on 12 March 1912. Although the only available illustration of it is taken from a Tiffany & Co. advertisement in *The Craftsman*, one can imagine the vivid colorations of the peacock, especially the tail feathers on the stem and foot. It is fitting that the cup

Tiffany showed a silver cup with transparent enamel decoration of peacocks at the 1915 Panama-Pacific Exposition in San Francisco. A photograph of it appeared in a Tiffany & Co. advertisement in *The Craftsman*, v. XXVI (April 1914), la.

Another object shown in San Francisco was this small copper bowl, its surface enameled in a roughened texture, with enameled maple seeds surrounding clusters of opals near the lip. *(Private collection)*.

is in the shape of a chalice, a vessel which holds the wine, symbolizing the blood of Christ in the Christian liturgy; in Christian art, the peacock is a symbol for immortality, a reference that Tiffany must have been aware of, since he employed this image in his ecclesiastical windows.

"Another piece is a cup of 18 karat gold covered with richly chased design of Indian ornament. This cup is elaborately pierced and filled with transparent enamels of rich blue and turquoise, the same tones being repeated in the ornament on the foot."[34] The body and foot of this cup (or bowl) are decorated with plique-à-jour enameling, achieved by piercing the gold and filling the area with enameling. According to a Tiffany & Co. pattern book, this cup (18194) was finished on 13 July 1913. The manufacturing charge was $2,500. (This is not a retail price but just the cost of fabrication, including materials and labor.) The entry also states that it was "enameled at store," which would indicate that the body of the cup was made in the silver division in New Jersey and subsequently enameled in New York under the direction of Julia Munson. The cup is stamped with the special exhibition mark, ¶P12. Henry Walters bought this piece at the exhibition and it is now in the Walters Art Gallery.[35]

"A tea screen completes the display. It is made out of a solid gold piece of 18 karat gold pierced and filled with translucent enamel. The frame is of 18 karat gold set in a base of carved boxwood."[36] This item, like the "Four Seasons" box, was based on a window that Tiffany had exhibited at an international exhibition; in this case, it was the "Parakeets and Goldfish Bowl" window that he had shown in the "Dark Room" at the 1893 World's Columbian Exposition in Chicago. He also selected this window to be illustrated in a promotional brochure for the exhibition.[37] In the window, parakeets are perched on branches of a blossoming fruit tree, from which a goldfish bowl is suspended.[38] The tea screen duplicates the image in the window with the exception of a spider web in the lower left-hand corner, added to fill in the expanse of the background space which could not have been enameled without metal supports. This was achieved by the cloisonné technique or gate wiring in which the web-like structure was soldered together. In order to replicate the image on the window, the craftsman pierced a sheet of gold, filling in the open areas with transparent enamel. Backing secured the enamel during firing which, when removed, allowed light to shine through, imitating the effect of the window. The tea screen is an enameling tour de force, using plique-à-jour enameling in the background areas, opaque enameling on the chain, fish bowl rim and spider web, transparent enameling in the tank, and translucent enameling on the branches. Since so many types of enameling were used, it was necessary to fire the areas with the metal supports first; the plique-à-jour enameling came later.[39] The tea screen is marked "Tiffany & Co. ¶P7".

81

83

According to two official catalogues, which listed all the exhibits in the Department of Fine Arts building for the Panama-Pacific Exposition, Louis Tiffany also exhibited a hand-wrought vase and a silver vase that were not included in *The Jewelers' Circular* article.[40] Along with the holloware objects, he showed a few pieces of jewelry:

A pendant with star fish as motif is made of Mexican opal matrix set in a finely chased body of 18 karat gold. Next to this is a necklace of two gold snakes, the entire body consisting of tiny enameled scales each of which is separately linked, so that the whole thing is flexible. The snakes are holding a large cabochon Ceylon sapphire. A spray of blackberries is also included. The upper four berries are made of carved garnets, coral and carnelian. The lower ones are of chased gold enameled to represent the unripe fruit. The leaves are of 18 karat gold pierced and filled with enamel.[41]

This last piece seems to resemble the blackberry spray that Tiffany showed in the 1904 St. Louis exhibition but with a few differences. Unlike the earlier spray, which is made of silver, this one is 18 karat gold and the leaves are plique-à-jour enameled. Not included in the *Jewelers' Circular* article was a spray of mistletoe "with leaves of carved jade and berries of unpolished moonstone."[42] These pieces would have been made in Tiffany's New York department. Like the silver and gold holloware objects, they would also have been stamped with the special Panama-Pacific marks.

    As mentioned above, at least one object was sold at the exposition; the 18 karat gold plique-à-jour cup bought by Henry Walters, an astute collector of fine works of art. Reviews stated that the Tiffany exhibit was greatly admired and "attracted much attention."[43] Ben Macomber, whose articles about the exhibition for *The San Francisco Chronicle* were published in book form, was particularly impressed with Tiffany's display: "the visitor will be struck by the small but exquisite exhibit in gold, enamel and precious stones of Louis C. Tiffany."[44] Louis Tiffany received a gold medal for his participation, a credit solely to his work in precious metals and jewelry.[45]

    After the exposition, Tiffany continued to work on jeweled and enameled objects but on a more selective basis. He designed two 3-piece tête-à-tête sets in May 1916, with consecutive numbers 19083 and 19084. Notations on drawings for both sets indicate that they were made specially for him. On the

81

This is the mark on the underside of the tea screen in Ill. 83. Unlike most Tiffany & Co. holloware which is stamped, this mark is hand engraved. The frame was soldered together around the tea screen, and stamping it in the traditional way would have damaged the delicate enamel work.

drawings for the teapot, sugar and creamer No. 19083, "Special work for Mr. Tiffany" is written in red ink, while a separate note, attached with a straight pin to the teapot drawing for 19084, states "3 Piece Tea Set (made from Mr. L. C. Tiffany's sketch)." These are the only two drawings in the Tiffany & Co. archives that I have seen with such a notation. It is possible that they were ordered by Tiffany for his personal use.[46]

The set 19083 is made of silver with ten vertical panels on the teapot, the upper section of each panel decorated with a five-petaled stylized floral pattern. Although a notation on the drawing mentions enameling, it does not specify whether the flowers were enameled or left silver-colored. Black outlining accentuates the foliate design while the insulators and fluted finial were made of coral. If the colors on this set follow the drawing, contrasts of silver with black enamel and red coral on the handle and knob are colors associated with the Art Deco movement. In fact, the shapes of the three pieces are very much in the modern taste; the bodies gradually taper from the lid to the domed foot.

The set 19084 is made of copper with enameled blue lozenge-shaped panels encircling the neck and foot, and with joining bands made up of six paneled sections, each set with eight amethysts, mounted in gold bezels. A crowning amethyst serves as the finial on both the teapot and sugar. The bodies of all three pieces were oxidized very darkly to give a rich patina to the surface. A notation on the upper right-hand corner of the drawing instructed the silverware division to "send order with spinning to store. Store will do soldering and will make mounts." This set, like 19083, was spun in the New Jersey silverware factory and sent to New York for assembling.

In 1916, Tiffany created an 18 karat gold cup (number 19132) that closely resembles ecclesiastical chalices from the medieval period.[47] A notation on the drawing states that it was made in the sixth-floor jewelry department in December 1916. The decorative motif on the cup is a restrained Byzantinesque pattern, executed in plique-à-jour enameling. According to a notation on the drawing, it was made with a "copper form over which to build filigree," indicating that a copper base in the shape of the cup was made over which the gold cloisons were formed. After firing, the copper backing was removed. The delicate cup is supported by four armatures, joined at the lip and creating the illusion that it is floating within its framework. Alternating cabochon amethysts and jade encircle the rim and foot and are studded along the armatures, complemented by larger pieces on the stem. This cup, like the one with "Indian ornament", was bought by Henry Walters.[48]

84

The last year when Tiffany devoted time to the jeweled objects produced at Tiffany & Co. seems to have been 1916. I know of only a few items designed after that year. One is a small gold oval jewel box in the shape of a snuff box, pattern number 19842, the drawing dated 21 October 1922. The central cartouche is decorated with an impressionistic figure of a dancing woman with her head thrown back and her right arm and right leg both raised, the whole executed in transparent enameling.

By 1918, Tiffany was devoting his energies to his next creative endeavor, the formation of the Tiffany Foundation. On 10 June of that year he submitted a letter of resignation as Art Director of Tiffany & Co: "As explained by Mr. de Forest I have decided to resign as Art Director of Tiffany & Co. Will ask you to present my resignation at the next meeting of the Board. I will be glad to continue as director & vice pres. of the Co. but without salary." Tiffany's resignation was accepted "with regret" at a special meeting of the Board of Directors on 18 June.[49] He continued to serve as Director, Vice-President and Assistant-Treasurer but no longer played a significant role at Tiffany & Co., although his jewelry and enameling department remained open until his death in 1933.

The Tiffany Foundation officially opened on 1 May 1920 with eight students.[50] Tiffany donated Laurelton Hall, with all its contents, to the Foundation, as well as a sizable endowment. Students were invited to spend from one to two months pursuing their art with the aim of stimulating their "imagination and the love of beauty by giving free play to the individuality of the artist . . . Laurelton, with its ponds and its many acres of gardens and woodland, situated on the shores of a beautiful harbor, is peculiarly adapted to such study."[51] Artists from both the fine and applied arts were invited, including painters, sculptors, etchers, jewelers, metal workers, landscape architects, and decorators. According to a brochure published by the Foundation in 1932, one silversmith and fourteen jewelers had studied at Laurelton Hall from its inception until the date of that publication. Edward E. Oakes, from the Boston Arts and Crafts Society, is the only jeweler of note among the list of students.[52]

To celebrate his 68th birthday, Tiffany assembled in 1916 a retrospective of his work, held at the Tiffany Studios at 345 Madison Avenue in New York. This exhibition featured his art, dating as early as 1869, and included precious objects he had designed and had made at Tiffany & Co. There were 142 paintings, while his "metal, glass, jewelry, enamels, and pottery"[53] were arranged in showcases as follows: No. 141, enamels on copper; 142, enamels on silver and copper; 143, latest work in favrile glass; 144, favrile glass; 145, mother-of-pearl, favrile glass and metal; 146, jewelry exhibited at the San Francisco Exposition; 147, gold vase ornamented with jewels exhibited at San Francisco; 148, glass; 149, enamels; 151, enamels on silver ornamented with precious stones, exhibited at San Francisco; and 151, pottery.[54] An article in the *New York Herald* clarifies a few of these items which had been exhibited in the Panama-

Pacific Exposition. "A silver gilt vase set with precious stones" is the large enameled vase with a center border of horns of plenty and pierced handles. It was exhibited behind the sofa in case 147. The silver jar with the frieze decorations of ''Flora'' and ''Ceres'' and the tea screen were probably included in case 150. The jewelry case 146 contained the four articles from the San Francisco exhibition.[55]

Tiffany included articles in his retrospective that he considered his true artistic achievements. Although his paintings had not been given the credit that he felt they deserved, he considered them true works of art, evidenced by the number he included in this exhibition. By 1916, Tiffany had amassed 115 pieces of his earlier enamels on copper for his personal collection, a selection of which he showed in this exhibition.

Tiffany chose the title, ''The Art Work of Louis C. Tiffany,'' to epitomize the carefully selected objects he included in his exhibition. That is the same title he had chosen for the book ghostwritten on his behalf by Charles DeKay two years earlier. As with most of his artistic endeavors, he seemed to know precisely what he wanted to create and how to realize his designs. Was he arrogantly strutting his magnificent stuff, like a proud peacock?

It is probably not a coincidence that the last known object created 80 by this genial artist is a plique-à-jour gold chalice enameled with peacock feathers, which he designed in 1925. This piece crystallizes the essence of Tiffany's art. Its cup is exquisitely shaped like a tulip, a gentle reminder of his unwavering admiration for the beauty of nature. It is executed to perfection using a very difficult enameling technique. The subtle peacock motif, evident in all phases of his art, may have been his last appeal to immortality.

Notes

Chapter 1

1 After the death of Charles L. Tiffany, his shares in the Allied Arts Company were divided between Louis Comfort Tiffany and his sister, Annie O. Mitchell. This exchange took place on 23 April 1902, on which date Louis Tiffany received eighteen bonds, totaling $14,750, while Annie Mitchell received fourteen for a total of $14,000. In addition, 84 shares of capital stock were divided equally between them. (Taken from a letter in the Tiffany Archives, addressed to Henry W. DeForest, Esq., 30 Broad Street, New York, dated 23 April 1902.)

2 Gertrude Speenburgh, *The Arts of the Tiffanys*, Chicago 1956, p. 33.

3 *The Evening Post*, 2 November 1907 (clipping from Archives of American Art microfilm: 1. Scrapbook 01-249, p. 50).

4 Michael John Burlingham, *The Last Tiffany: A Biography of Dorothy Tiffany Burlingham*, New York 1989, p. 12.

5 Joseph Purtell, *The Tiffany Touch*, New York 1971, p. 16.

6 The Tiffanys' first son, Charles Lewis, was born on 7 October 1842 but lived only 4½ years.

7 Up to this period, Tiffany had been retailing the flatware of other manufacturers such as John Polhamus, Henry Hebbard, and Gorham & Co., usually double hallmarking the maker's mark with the Tiffany & Co. stamp.

8 Michael John Burlingham, *op. cit.*, p. 40.

9 I have been able to locate only one drawing in the Tiffany & Co. archives which Moore copied directly from a source. On etching design No. 545 for tea caddy, pattern No. 4824, dated 1 June 1881, a notation at the bottom instructs the etcher to "refer to Grammar of Ornament for second etching." Upon examining Jones's book, we find that the plant design is taken from Plate XCIX. I would like to thank Ruth Caccavale, my former assistant in the Tiffany archives, for bringing this drawing to my attention while she was organizing the archival material in preparation for microfilming.

10 Although all the pieces exhibited at this exhibition were designed under the direction of John Curran, the drawing for the Indian bowl was initialed by Edward C. Moore, indicating that he approved this design just before he died on 2 August 1891, a full two years before the exhibition took place.

11 Gertrude Speenburgh, *op. cit.*, p. 87.

12 Doreen Bolger Burke, "Louis Comfort Tiffany and His Early Training at Eagleswood, 1862–1865," *The American Journal of Art*, Vol. XIX, No. 3 (1987), 29.

13 *Ibid.*, 35.

14 *Ibid.*, 34.

15 *Ibid.*, 32.

16 *Ibid.*, 32.

17 *Ibid.*, 30.

18 *Ibidem*.

19 Charles DeKay, *The Art of Louis Comfort Tiffany*, New York 1914, p. 7.

20 Charles and Mary Grace Carpenter, *Tiffany Silver*, New York 1978, pp. 12–13.

21 Michael John Burlingham, *op. cit.*, p. 41.

22 Gary A. Reynolds, *Louis Comfort Tiffany: The Paintings*, exhibition held at the Grey Art Gallery and Study Center, New York University, 20 March–12 May 1979, p. 8.

23 Charles DeKay, *op. cit.*, p. 5

24 Gary A. Reynolds, *op. cit.*, p. 13.

25 Charles DeKay, *op. cit.*, p. 8.

26 Quoted by Louis Comfort Tiffany in "Colour and its Kinship to Sound," Address before the Rembrandt Club of Brooklyn, *The Art World*, II, No. 2 (May 1917), 142.

27 Hugh F. McKean, *The "Lost" Treasures of Louis Comfort Tiffany*, New York 1980, p. 3.

28 S. Bing, "Louis C. Tiffany's Coloured Glass Work," *Exhibition of L'Art Nouveau*, Paris 1899, p. 11.

29 Gertrude Speenburgh, *op. cit.*, p. 85.

30 Faude, Wilson H., "Associated Artists and the American Renaissance in the Decorative Arts," *Winterthur Portfolio*, 10 (1975), 107.

31 Brownell, William C., "Decoration of the Seventh Regiment Armory," *Scribner's Monthly*, Vol. 22, No 3 (July 1881), 375.

32 Garance Aufaure, "A Masterpiece of American Renaissance," *Vogue Decoration*, No. 22 (October, November 1989), 106.

33 Quoted in "Mr. Tiffany's Speech at his Birthday Breakfast, Saturday, February 19, 1916," p. 4. I would like to thank Paula and Howard Ellman for sharing this document with me.

34 Louis Comfort Tiffany, *op. cit.*, p. 143.

35 From minutes of Board of Directors meetings, *1868–1908 Records No. 1 T & Co.*, 7 June 1881, n.p.

36 Saarinen, Aline B., *The Proud Possessors*, New York 1958, p. 157.

37 Hugh F. McKean, *op. cit.*, p. 138.

38 "Tiffany Glass and Decorating Company's Exhibit at the Columbian Exposition," *The*

Decorator and Furnisher, Vol. 23, No. 1 (October 1893), 10.

39 Herwin Schaefer, "Tiffany's Fame in Europe," *The Art Bulletin*, Vol. 44, No. 4 (December 1962), 313.

40 "Tiffany Glass and Decorating Company's Exhibit . . .", *op. cit.*, 11; and a brochure, *A Synopsis of the Exhibit of the Tiffany Glass and Decorating Company in the American Section of the Manufactures and Liberal Arts Building at the World's Fair*, privately printed by Tiffany Glass & Decorating Company, New York 1893, n.p.

41 For illustration, see William Feldstein, Jr. and Alastair Duncan, *The Lamps of Tiffany Studios*, New York 1983, p. 97.

42 For illustration, see Janet Zapata, "The Rediscovery of Paulding Farnham: Tiffany's Designer Extraordinaire," *The Magazine Antiques*, Vol. 139, No. 3 (March 1991), 556–67.

43 Henri Vever, *Rapport officiel de l'Exposition internationale de Chicago en 1893. Comité 24. Bijouterie-Joaillerie*, Paris 1894, p. 67.

Chapter 2

1 S. Bing, *Artistic America*, reprint, Cambridge, Mass., 1970, p. 146.

2 Quoted from Martin Eidelberg in Alastair Duncan, Martin Eidelberg, and Neil Harris, *Masterworks of Louis Comfort Tiffany*, London/ New York 1989, p. 77.

3 *Ibid.*, p. 157.

4 Hugh F. McKean, *op. cit.*, p. 237.

5 Lewis F. Day, *Enamelling, A Comparative Account of the Development and Practice of the Art*, London 1907, p. 2.

6 Himilce Novas, "A Jewel in His Crown," *Connoisseur*, Vol. 213, No. 860 (October 1983), 135.

7 According to Robert Koch, *Rebel In Glass* (3rd edition), New York 1982, p. 136, Alice Gouvy took charge of the department in 1903. Her becoming the director of this division coincided with Julia Munson's leaving the department to establish Tiffany's artistic jewelry department, originally located at Tiffany's mansion at 72nd Street.

8 I would like to thank Martin Eidelberg for this information, which was provided to him during an interview with Julia Munson Sherman.

9 Robert Koch, *Louis C. Tiffany's Glass-Bronzes-Lamps: A Complete Collector's Guide*, New York 1971, p. 113.

10 Robert Koch, *ibid.*, pp. 113–14, illustrates a letter, dated 9 November 1921, from A. Douglas Nash, manager of Tiffany Furnaces, to Ms. Gay, informing her that he has installed a department for enameling and would like her to return to help out.

11 Himilce Novas, *op. cit.*, p. 134 and Gertrude Speenburgh, *op. cit.*, p. 79.

12 Mrs. Nelson Dawson, *Enamels*, London 1906, pp. 5–6.

13 H. H. Cunynghame, *On the Theory and Practice of Art-Enamelling upon Metals*, Westminster 1901, pp. 2–3. Gertrude Speenburgh, *op. cit.*, p. 75, itemizes an almost identical list of oxides that were used in Tiffany's workshop.

14 Alexander Fisher's "how-to" articles were not the first to be published on this subject in England. During the first decade of the 20th century, several other books appeared which dealt with enameling history and techniques, written by practitioners in the field. Henry H. Cunynghame of the Home Department wrote *European Enamels*, which includes a chapter on techniques but is mostly devoted to the history of enameling in Europe from ancient times to the first decade of the 20th century, and *On the Theory and Practice of Art-Enameling Upon Metals* devoted to the principles and manufacture of enamels. Lewis F. Day, a designer and a prolific writer on design subjects, wrote *Enamelling* (see fn. 5 above), whose subject is self-evident from the title. Prominent enamelers such as Nelson Dawson and his wife, Edith, who collaborated on jewelry and silver, each wrote a book. Nelson Dawson's *Goldsmiths' and Silversmiths' Work* touches upon the subject of enameling within the context of jewelry and silver while Mrs. Dawson in *Enamels* deals with the history and various techniques of enameling. The jeweler Henry Wilson includes a chapter on enameling in *Silverwork and Jewellery*.

15 Alexander Fisher, *The Art of Enamelling on Metals*, London 1906, pp. 33–35.

16 Henry H. Cunynghame, *European Enamels*, London 1906, p. 7.

17 Samuel Howe, "Enamel as a Decorative Agent," *The Craftsman*, Vol. II, No. 2 (May 1902), 64–65.

18 Cunynghame, *op. cit.*, pp. 11–12.

19 Tiffany enamels were advertised in *Art Interchange*, Vol. 50, No. 5 (May 1903), n.p., and in the 1904 Tiffany & Co. *Blue Book*, pp. 375–76. *Blue Books* were the firm's yearly catalogues which were distributed to preferred customers. They were issued late in the preceding year, probably in time for holiday shopping.

20 Quoted from advertisement for Tiffany Studios, "Interior Furnishings in Special and Unique Designs," *Art Interchange*, Vol. 50, No. 5 (May 1903), n.p.

21 For a list of the enamelware in Tiffany's collection at Laurelton Hall, see auction catalogue, Parke-Bernet Galleries, *The Objects of Art of the Louis Comfort Tiffany Foundation*, 24–28 September 1946, lots 298–326.

22 Tiffany & Co., *Blue Book*, 1904, pp. 375–76.

23 Samuel Howe, *op. cit.*, p. 64.

24 Henry W. Belknap, ''Jewellery and Enamels,'' *The Craftsman*, Vol. IV, No. 3 (June 1903), 179.

25 Tiffany & Co., *Blue Book*, 1904, p. 375.

26 The assumptions that I am setting forth are based on those objects which I have been able to examine. As additional Tiffany enamelware becomes available, my suppositions may have to be revised.

27 It is hoped that as more objects come to light and can be related to specific drawings, this hypothesis will be reconfirmed.

28 This vase was illustrated in a review of the Turin World's Fair. For illustration, see ''Die Turiner Ausstellung: Die Sektion Amerika,'' *Dekorative Kunst*, Vol. 11 (October 1902), 55.

29 I would like to thank David Donaldson at the Charles Hosmer Morse Museum of American Art for his helpful insights into the technique of iridescence. Quoted from Hugh Weir, ''Through the Rooking Glass,'' *Collier's*, Vol. 75, No. 21 (23 May 1925), 51.

30 For illustration, see Robert Judson Clark, *The Arts and Crafts Movement in America 1876–1916*, Princeton 1972, p. 23.

31 The nature sketches of peppers and pumpkin vines are in the collection of the Charles Hosmer Morse Museum of American Art, Winter Park, Florida.

32 I have seen only one variation on this theme within this series, a waisted cylindrical vase, the upper section pierced with leafage and some type of pods in iridescent shades of green, salmon, rust and amber. For illustration, see Sotheby's catalogue, ''Important Tiffany and Other Art Nouveau'', 24 March 1984, lot No. 169, and Alastair Duncan, *Tiffany at Auction*, New York 1981, p. 52, illustration No. 144.

33 For illustration, see Alastair Duncan, *Louis Comfort Tiffany*, New York 1992, p. 96.

34 *The Objects of Art of the Louis Comfort Tiffany Foundation, Laurelton Hall*, lot No. 322.

35 For illustration of the Jack-in-the-pulpit and the corn pottery vases, see John Loring, *Tiffany's 150 Years*, New York 1987, pp. 122–23. For illustration of Jack-in-the-pulpit pottery vase with bisque finish, see Alastair Duncan, Martin Eidelberg and Neil Harris, *op. cit.*, p. 82 and Hugh F. McKean, *op. cit.*, p. 206.

36 I would like to thank David Donaldson at the Charles Hosmer Morse Museum of American Art for his helpful suggestions about this vase.

37 For illustration, see Hugh F. McKean, *op. cit.*, p. 240, figure 235. The mark on this bowl is SG123 which indicates that it was made after his experimentation with the vase form. Along with the SG mark, the piece has also been marked ''162 A-Coll'' which indicated that Tiffany kept this item in his Laurelton Hall collection.

38 For illustration, see Sotheby's catalogue, ''Important Tiffany and Other Art Nouveau'', 24 March 1984, lot No. 170. I am not aware of any Tiffany enamels in the SG series with numbers from 124 to 161. Perhaps as more of these enamels become known, the gap will be filled in with another as yet unknown group.

39 For an illustration of this covered box, see Sotheby's catalogue, ''Important Tiffany and Other Art Nouveau'', *op. cit.*, lot No. 170.

40 I have not examined this vase. When it was illustrated in the catalogue for the Burt Sugarman collection at Christie's, 30 March 1985, lot No. 2, the caption noted that it was impressed SG282. Sotheby's catalogue, ''20th Century Decorative Arts'', March 11, 1989, lot No. 609, records an identical vase as SG 232. I believe that this is the same vase and feel that the earlier number is the correct mark. Marks are often hard to decipher; 3s do look like 8s. Since Tiffany was producing covered boxes where the last known number is SG 208, it would seem logical that the next group would have begun within twenty to thirty numbers from this last number.

41 For illustration, see ''Die Turiner Ausstellung . . .'', *loc. cit.*

42 Horace Townsend, ''American and French Applied Art at the Grafton Galleries,'' *The International Studios*, Vol. 8 (July 1899), 43.

43 I would like to thank Katie Leong and Jean Lichtenstein for their helpful suggestions regarding the creation of this box.

44 The box with the flowering dogwood branches over favrile glass is located at the shop of Lillian Nassau Ltd., New York.

45 For an illustration of this covered jar, see Sotheby's catalogue, ''Important Art Nouveau and Art Deco'', 17 November 1984, lot No. 264. A similar ovoid jar is illustrated in *The Objects of Art of the Louis Comfort Tiffany Foundation, Laurelton Hall*, lot No. 314, p. 247.

46 For illustration of this covered box, see Sotheby's catalogue, ''Important Tiffany and Other Art Nouveau'', *op. cit.*, lot No. 167.

47 For illustration, see Christie's catalogue, ''Fine Art Nouveau and Art Deco'', 30 March 1985, lot No. 386.

48 For illustration, see microfilm, Archives of American Art Smithsonian-Louis Comfort Tiffany Scrapbook, 01-249, p. 55.

49 Document in the Tiffany & Co. archives, dated 21 November 1902.

50 I would like to thank Jonathan Snellenburg for his help in sorting out the enameling techniques that Tiffany used in this series.

51 Stuart P. Feld, ''Nature in Her Most Seductive Aspect: Louis Comfort Tiffany's Favrile Glass,'' *Bulletin of the Metropolitan Museum of Art*, Vol.

21 (November 1962), 103. In 1951, the Louis Comfort Tiffany Foundation formally changed this loan into a gift to the Museum.

52 For illustration of vase number 14, see Christie's catalogue, "Highly Important Tiffany: The Burt Sugarman Collection", 30 March 1985, lot No. 1. The vase marked with number 19 is in the collection of the Charles Hosmer Morse Museum of American Art.

53 According to a pamphlet, "Jewelery & Enamels Exhibited at the Louisiana Purchase Exposition, Saint Louis, Missouri, April 30th to November 30th 1904," Tiffany exhibited the following enamels on copper: vase 100, vase 48, vase 187, bowl 112, and vase 251. The vase in the collection of the Metropolitan Museum of Art is bowl number 112. The illustration of this vase/bowl appears in Charles DeKay, *op. cit.*, plate following p. 32.

54 For illustration, see Sotheby's catalogue, "Important Tiffany and Other Art Nouveau", *op. cit.*, lots Nos. 164 and 165. According to Robert Koch, *op. cit.*, p. 56, an 'X' on the underside of a piece of favrile glass indicates that it was an experimental piece.

55 For illustration, see Hugh F. McKean, *op.cit.*, Figure 234, p. 239.

56 For illustration, see Alastair Duncan, Martin Eidelberg and Neil Harris, *op. cit.*, illustrations 14, 15.

57 *The Objects of Art of the Louis Comfort Tiffany Foundation, Laurelton Hall, op. cit.*; inkstand, lot No. 312, letter rack, lot No. 321.

58 For illustration, see Hugh F. McKean, *op. cit.*, Figure 234, p. 239.

59 For illustration, see *The Objects of Art of the Louis Comfort Tiffany Foundation, op. cit.*, lot No. 316, p. 247. For color illustration, see Alastair Duncan, Martin Eidelberg and Neil Harris, *op. cit.*, Illustration No. 12.

60 For illustration, see John Loring, *op. cit.*, p. 69.

61 From *1919 Inventory of Laurelton Hall*, M. M. Frederick Savage (October 1919) copied by John E. Terwilliger (January 1937), p. 33.

62 For illustration, see M. P. Verneuil, "The Insect in Decoration," *The Craftsman*, Vol. V, No. 6 (March 1904), 563.

63 Gertrude Speenburgh visited Laurelton Hall, taking many photographs which she included in her book. For illustration of the cabinet containing the cicada box, see *The Arts of the Tiffanys, op. cit.*, p. 76. I would like to thank Frederick Brandt, curator of Twentieth Century Decorative Arts at the Virginia Museum of Fine Arts for calling my attention to this illustration.

64 For illustration, see Hugh F. McKean, *op. cit.*, Figure 235, p. 240.

65 See *The Objects of Art of the Louis Comfort Tiffany Foundation, op cit.*, lot No. 309.

66 Gardner Teall, "Artistic American Wares at Exposition," *Brush and Pencil*, Vol. 6, No. 4 (July 1900), 180; Dr. Gensel, "Tiffany-Gläser auf der Pariser Welt-Ausstellung 1900," *Deutsche Kunst und Dekoration*, Vol. VI (November 1900), 91; and Roger Marx, *La Décoration et les Industries d'art à l'exposition universelle de 1900*, Paris 1901, p. 105. I would like to thank Sheldon Barr for calling this review to my attention.

67 See Gardner Teall, *op. cit.*, p. 180.

68 For illustration, see Charles DeKay, *op. cit.*, facing p. 35 and *The Objects of Art of the Louis Comfort Tiffany Foundation, op. cit.*, lot No. 313, p. 247.

69 For illustration, see Samuel Howe, *op. cit.*, p. 60.

70 For illustration, see "The Tiffany Glass at the Pan American," *Keramic Studio*, Vol. III, No. 2 (June 1901), 31.

71 For illustration of another version of the dandelion lamp, see William Feldstein Jr. and Alastair Duncan, *op. cit.*, p. 145. Dandelion leaves and puff balls decorate the base but do not continue around the top. I feel that this lamp was made later.

72 *The Jewelers Review*, 24 July 1901, p. 177 is a review of the Allied Arts Co.'s exhibit. An entire case contained the new 'lustre' enamels which they proclaim as "the first lustre enamel productions ever exhibited."

73 Quoted from Gardner C. Teall, "The Art of Things," *Brush and Pencil*, Vol. 4 (September 1899), 310.

74 This version was not executed with the three peacock heads which would have hidden the favrile glass with peacock feather decoration. For illustration, see William Feldstein, Jr. and Alastair Duncan, *op. cit.*, p. 61.

75 Tiffany reacquired the peacock lamp, displaying it in his exhibition held at the Tiffany Studios showrooms to celebrate his sixty-eighth birthday in 1916. Tiffany retained this lamp for his collection, housed at Laurelton Hall and included it in the 1919 inventory. At Laurelton Hall, it was displayed in the second-floor gallery and was listed as "Peacock Banquet Lamp." (From *1919 Inventory of Laurelton Hall, op. cit.*, p. 33.) It was also listed among items offered for sale at the Tiffany Foundation Laurelton Hall sale in 1946, lot No. 288.

76 Quoted in "Exhibition Notes," *The China Decorator*, Vol. 25, No. 4 (April 1900), 92.

77 "The Tiffany Glass at the Pan American," *op. cit.*, 31. An illustration of the dandelion lamp also appeared on the same page.

78 Tiffany exhibited an enameled box and jar at an arts and crafts exhibition at the Art Institute of Chicago. See *Catalogue of the First Annual Exhibition of Original Designs for Decorations and*

Examples of Art Crafts having Distinct Artistic Merit, 16 December 1902 to 11 January 1903, item numbers 668 and 669, p. 55. I would like to thank Rosalie Berberian for sharing this information with me. For more information on the Turin Exposition, see ''Die Turiner Ausstellung . . .'', *op. cit.*, 49–55; *Esposizione d'Arte Decorativa Moderna Torino 1902 Tiffany Studios*, 1–15; ''American Art at the Turin Exposition,'' *The Jewelers' Circular and Horological Review*, Vol. XLV, No. 8 (24 September 1902), 1, 18, (continued to 22 October 1902), 48–49. Tiffany exhibited the following enamels on copper in the 1904 St. Louis Lousiana Purchase Exposition: vase with enameled hawk, vase with enameled mushrooms, vase with enameled berries, and two enameled vases. (Taken from booklet, ''Tiffany & Co. Louisiana Purchase Exposition Saint Louis 1904'', p. 7.) Two enamels on copper which Tiffany exhibited in the 1906 Paris Salon are illustrated in *L'Art décoratif aux salons 1906*, microfilm, Archives of American Art Smithsonian-Louis Comfort Tiffany Scrapbook, 01-249, p. 55.

Chapter 3

1 See *1868–1908 Records No. 1 T & Co.*, 14 March 1902, n.p. (Tiffany & Co. Archives).
2 *Ibid.*, 22 March 1902, n.p. (Tiffany & Co. Archives).
3 *Ibid.*, 6 June and 5 December 1905, n.p. (Tiffany & Co. Archives).
4 For illustration see Charles and Mary Grace Carpenter, *op. cit.*, p. 123.
5 Information received directly from John Farnham; see Janet Zapata, ''The Rediscovery of Paulding Farnham, Tiffany's Designer Extraordinaire – Part II: Silver,'' *The Magazine Antiques*, Vol. 139, No. 4 (April 1991), 725–26, illustration on 729.
6 For illustration of Paulding Farnham's silver and jewelry designed for the 1904 Louisiana Purchase Exposition in St. Louis, see ''Tiffany and Company at the Saint Louis Exposition,'' *The Craftsman*, Vol. VII, No. 2 (November 1904), 171–75.
7 Gertrude Speenburgh, *op. cit.*, p. 74.
8 *Ibid.*, p. 74.
9 *Ibid.*, p. 74.
10 Although Julia Munson Sherman does not specify that she is referring to only those pieces of jewelry made from 1902 to 1907, an approximation of the amount of jewelry Louis Tiffany produced at Tiffany & Co. reveals that he made about 5,500 pieces from 1907 to 1933. I feel that Mrs Sherman is confusing the two departments and referring only to those pieces made at Tiffany Furnaces. See Himilce Novas, *op. cit.*, 138.
11 Quoted from ''Tiffany and Company, at the Saint Louis Exposition,'' *The Craftsman*, Vol. VII,

No. 2 (November 1904), 182.
12 Taken from pamphlet, *Tiffany & Co. Louisiana Purchase Exposition, Saint Louis 1904*, privately printed by Tiffany & Co., 1904, Nos. 15, 18 and 19, pp. 5, 6.
13 For illustration, see Alastair Duncan, Martin Eidelberg, and Neil Harris, *op. cit.*, p. 84.
14 ''Tiffany and Company'', *op. cit.*, 182–83.
15 *Ibid.*, 182.
16 ''The Jeweler's Craft: New Ideas in the Art which makes use of Precious Gems and Metals,'' *Washington Life*, Vol. III. No. 19 (5 November 1904), 18.
17 *Ibidem.*
18 For more information and the quotation, see Hugh F. McKean, *op. cit.*, pp. 251–54.
19 ''Notable Exhibits at the St. Louis Exposition: Part 1 – Jewelry, by L. C. Tiffany,'' *The Jewelers' Circular-Weekly*, Vol. 49, No. 13 (26 October 1904), 18.
20 ''Louis C. Tiffany and His Work in Artistic Jewellery,'' *The International Studio*, Vol. 30, No. 117 (November 1906), xxxiv.
21 For illustration, see *L'Art Décoratif aux Salons de 1906 Bijouterie-Orfèvrerie-Ornamentation*, Première Serie, Plates 88–89.
22 Quoted in ''Tiffany and Company'', *op. cit.*, 183.
23 See pamphlet, *Tiffany & Co. Louisiana Purchase Exposition Saint Louis 1904, op. cit.*, p. 6; Charles DeKay, *op. cit.* p. 33.
24 For illustration, see *L'Art décoratif aux Salons de 1906, op. cit.*, Plates 88–89.
25 See *Art Property from the Estate of the Late Mrs. Henry Walters*, Parke-Bernet Galleries, Inc., 30 November and 1, 2, 3 and 4 December 1943, lot No. 586, p. 102.
26 Quoted in ''Notable Exhibits at the St. Louis Exposition,'' *op. cit.*, p. 20; and ''Tiffany's St. Louis Exhibit,'' *The Boston Budget*, Vol. XXXIV, No. 47 (19 November 1904), 11.
27 Quoted in ''Tiffany and Company'', *op. cit.*, 183.
28 For illustration, see Alastair Duncan, Martin Eidelberg and Neil Harris, *op. cit.*, p. 85.
29 From *1919 Inventory of Laurelton Hall*, by M. M. Frederick Savage (October 1919), copied by John E. Terwilliger (January 1937), p. 37.
30 For illustration, see Susan Stronge, Nima Smith and J. C. Harle, *A Golden Treasury Jewellery from the Indian Subcontinent*, New York 1988, p. 60, pl. 48.
31 For reproduction see Thomas Holbein Hendley, *The Journal of Indian Art*, Vol. XII, No. 95–107, pl. CXXII. Hendley wrote a series of essays for this journal, dating from July 1906 to July 1909, devoted solely to Indian jewelry.
32 For illustration, see Christie's catalogue,

"Nineteenth Century Sculpture, American Arts and Crafts, Art Nouveau Furniture and Tiffany", 15 November 1980, lot No. 383.

33 Quoted from *A Synopsis of the Exhibit of the Tiffany Glass and Decorating Company in the American Section of the Manufacturers, and Liberal Arts Building at the World's Fair*, privately printed by Tiffany Glass & Decorating Company, 1893, p.12.

34 Hugh F. McKean, *op. cit.*, p. 249.

35 Charles DeKay, *op. cit.*, plate following p. 32.

36 See *The Mrs. Henry Walters Art Collection*, Volume One, Parke-Bernet Galleries, Inc., 23 to 26 April 1941, lot No. 487, p. 98.

Chapter 4

1 See *1868–1908 Records No. 1 T & Co.*, 15 February 1907, n.p. (Tiffany & Co. Archives).

2 I would like to thank Len Rothe for information about the life of Charles Cook. Mr. Rothe's upcoming book, *Tiffany & Co: Developer of Artistic Taste and Culture in America – The Untold Story of Charles Lewis Tiffany* (working title), will provide new information about Cook and his importance at Tiffany & Co.

3 See *1868–1909 Records No. 1 T & Co.*, 3 May 1907, n. p. (Tiffany & Co. Archives).

4 See *Tiffany & Co. Engagements*, Vol. 5 (1906), p. 82 (Tiffany & Co. Archives).

5 The above information can be found in *Tiffany & Co. Engagements*, Vols 5–10, 1906–1933 (Tiffany & Co. Archives).

6 For additional information, see Polly King, "Women Workers in Glass at the Tiffany Studios," *The Art Interchange*, Vol. 33, No. 4 (October 1894), 86–87. According to Cecilia Waern, Tiffany let all his workmen go after a strike, hiring young women from the art schools to replace them since he felt "they had at least learned to use their eyes and their fingers in certain ways.", "The Industrial Arts of America; The Tiffany Glass and Decorative Co." *The Studio: An Illustrated Magazine of the Fine and Applied Arts*, Vol. XI, No. 2 (September 1897), 157.

7 Polly King, *op. cit.*, 87.

8 Quoted in Tiffany & Co., *Blue Book*, Vol. 16, New York 1909, p. 618.

9 Charles DeKay, *op. cit.*, p. 35.

10 Cecilia Waern, *loc. cit.*

11 Quoted in Tiffany & Co., *Blue Book*, Vol. 16, New York 1909, p. 618.

12 Quoted in Tiffany & Co., *Blue Book*, Vol. 19, New York 1912, p. 566.

13 Himilce Novas, *op. cit.*, 138.

14 *Ibidem*.

15 Although the department had been acquired in 1907, it would have taken at least a year to produce a sufficient amount of stock to offer in a catalogue.

The *Blue Books* were assembled in the year prior to their distribution and were sent out in December, dated the following year; therefore, 1909 would have been the earliest date Louis's jewelry could have been offered.

16 For illustration, see *Tiffany & Co. Exhibit: Louisiana Purchase Exposition St. Louis 1904*, Neg. No. 2820. (Photographic scrapbook located in Tiffany & Co. archives).

17 "Louis C. Tiffany and His Work in Artistic Jewellery," *op. cit.*, xxxii.

18 From *1919 Inventory of Laurelton Hall, op. cit.*, pp. 36–38.

19 Quoted in Clement W. Coumbe, "The Ancient Egyptian Scarab – Its History and Symbolic Significance," *The Jewelers' Circular-Weekly*, Vol. 56, No. 22 (1 July 1908), 43–44.

20 Quoted in Leo A. Stone, "The Scarab," *The Jewelers' Circular-Weekly*, Vol. 73, No. 10 (4 October 1916), 63.

21 Percy E. Newberry, *Scarabs: An Introduction to the Study of Egyptian Seals and Signet Rings*, London 1906, p. 61.

22 From *1919 Inventory of Laurelton Hall, op. cit.*, pp. 36–37.

23 This necklace was in the possession of the Tiffany family. Dora Jane Janson, *From Slave to Siren: The Victorian Woman and Her Jewelry From Neoclassic to Art Nouveau*, Duke University Museum of Art, Durham, North Carolina (May 1971), 49.

24 For illustration, see Carol Andrews, *Ancient Egyptian Jewelry*, New York 1991, p. 176 or Milada Vilimkova, *Egyptian Jewellery*, London 1969, Plate 6. Although this necklace was not discovered until 1930, too late to have influenced Tiffany's beetle jewelry, Tiffany may have seen a similar piece during his travels abroad.

25 For illustration, see "Special and Fancy Pieces in Tiffany & Co.'s Exhibit," *The Jewelers' Weekly*, Vol. 16, No. 21 (16 August 1893), 23.

26 For illustration, see Marilyn Jenkins and Manuel Keene, *Islamic Jewelry in the Metropolitan Museum of Art*, New York 1982, Plate 71, p. 129.

27 For detailed description of how filigree is made, see Ruth and Max Fröhlich, *Filigran aus Cortina d'Ampezzo um die Jahrhundertwende*, Zurich 1980, pp. 9–52.

28 For illustration, see Sotheby Parke-Bernet catalogue, "Art Nouveau and Art Deco", 24 November 1978, lot No. 133.

29 For illustration, see Ronald Jessup, *Anglo-Saxon Jewellery*, New York 1953, Plates XXII and XXIII.

30 See J. Bertrand, "Le Bijou en 1904," *Revue de la bijouterie, joaillerie, orfèvrerie*, Vol. 4, No. 47 (March 1904), 383.

31 Illustrated in Janet Zapata, "The Rediscovery of Paulding Farnham, Tiffany's Designer

Extraordinaire, Part I,'' *op. cit.*, 563.

32 In the latter part of the 19th and early 20th centuries, certain flowers and plants were symbolic of virtues and vices.

33 William R. Johnston, ''Recent Additions to the Jewelry Collection,'' *The Walters Monthly Bulletin* (November 1991), 5.

34 From *1919 Inventory of Laurelton Hall*, *op. cit.*, pp. 37, 38.

35 For illustrtation, see Thomas Holbein Hendley, *op. cit.*, Plate 32, No. 219 and Plate 46, No. 316.

36 Durr Friedley, ''Oriental Decorative Art,'' *Bulletin of the Metropolitan Museum of Art*, Vol. X, No. 8 (August 1915), 160–67.

Chapter 5

1 Quoted in Samuel Howe, ''Enamel as a Decorative Agent,'' *op. cit.*, 65–66.

2 For a list of pattern numbers with dates, see Charles and Mary Grace Carpenter, *op. cit.*, pp. 260–61. These dates apply only to the time when that particular form was put into production. In many instances, Tiffany & Co. continued to produce the same form for many years, stamping the number on the underside. President's letter dates help to give an approximate date of manufacture.

3 The great French houses of Boucheron, Cartier and Mauboussin used only 18 karat gold in their jewelry, unlike many American firms whose jewelry was made of 14 karat gold. Tiffany & Co. considered themselves rivals to the French and proudly advertised their 18 karat gold jewelry. They continued to produce jewelry in 18 karat gold until the 1940s. I have found only one instance in which the firm used 14 karat gold in their jewelry creations, the jewelry reproduced from the Curium treasury, c. 1877.

4 See *Tiffany & Co. Engagements*, Vol. 6, 1912, p. 82 (Tiffany & Co. Archives).

5 See *Tiffany & Co. Engagements*, Vol. 5, 1906, p. 85 (Tiffany & Co. Archives).

6 For more information on Albert A. Southwick, see ''Artist and Silversmith – How One Man Worked to be a Successful Designer,'' *The Craftsman*, Vol. X (May 1906), 176–79. Southwick remained in the Tiffany & Co. silverware division until 20 May 1922 when he was transferred to the Tiffany & Co. branch in Paris. *Tiffany & Co. Engagements*, Vol. 7, 1917, p. 72.

7 For illustration, see Martin Eidelberg, *E. Colonna*, catalogue of an exhibition held at the Dayton Art Institute, Musée des arts décoratifs de Montréal, and the Renwick Gallery of the National Museum of American Art, 1984, p. 42, Fig. B.

8 As part of the Tiffany & Co. display at the 1900 Exposition Universelle in Paris they exhibited six vases, combining favrile glass and gold mountings,

set with the following gemstones: pink American tourmalines, aquamarines, tourmalines from Maine, American pearls, demantoid garnets, and American sapphires. They also contributed a vase with Tiffany favrile glass with two silver gold-plated mermaids supporting the vase, set with American pearls and aquamarines and a scent bottle (see Ill. 4). Catalogue: *Tiffany & Co.'s Exhibit Paris Exposition Universelle 1900* (Catalogue Proof), pp. 13–14. For illustration of Tiffany favrile glass vase with gold-plated mermaids, see Sotheby's catalogue, *Elton John Art Nouveau and Art Deco*, Vol. 3, London, 7 September 1988, lot No. 617. For illustration of vase with favrile glass mounted in gold with American pearls, see ''The Tiffany Display at Paris,'' *The Art Interchange*, Vol. 44, No. 5 (May 1900), 112.

9 For illustration of the inkwell in the Newark Museum, see Charles and Mary Grace Carpenter, *op. cit.*, p. 47 and for the one in Charles Hosmer Morse Museum of American Art, see Hugh F. McKean, *op. cit.*, p. 232, Fig. 231.

10 The inkwell in the Newark Museum is marked o8648 while the one in the Charles Hosmer Morse Museum of American Art is engraved o8476. See Martin Eidelberg, ''Tiffany's Early Glass Vessels,'' *The Magazine Antiques*, Vol. 137, No. 2 (February 1990), 510.

11 See 1907 Tiffany & Co. *Blue Book*, p. 531.

12 See Tiffany & Co. silver ledger (no title), 1904–1907, p. 58.

13 For illustration of this bowl, see Paul E. Doros, *The Tiffany Collection of the Chrysler Museum at Norfolk*, Norfolk 1978, p. 70, fig. 74. The bowl bears an inscription date of 1909.

14 1909 Tiffany & Co. *Blue Book*, p. 620. Inkstands were offered at prices from $100 to $225.

15 Charles Tiffany died on 17 February 1902 but it was not until the next Board of Trustees meeting on 14 March that Charles Cook was elected president and not until 29 December of that same year that the letter designation ''T'' for Charles Tiffany was changed to ''C'' for Charles Cook. For more information, see Tiffany ledger, 1868–1908 Records No. 1 T & Co., 29 December 1902.

16 Quoted in Alexander Fisher, *op. cit.*, p. 21.

17 See Tiffany & Co. 1911 *Blue Book*, pp. 613–14.

18 I would like to thank Katie Leong and Jean Lichtenstein for their helpful insights into the technique of plique-à-jour enameling.

19 For illustration, see O. Gerdeil, ''La Norvège à l'Exposition Universelle,'' *L'Art Décoratif*, Vol. 3, No. 1 (October 1900), 30–31. For more information about J. Tostrup as well as additional illustrations of his plique-à-jour vessels, see Thor Kielland, *Om Gullsmedkunst I Hundre Ar*, Oslo 1932, pp. 261–63, Plates 73–75.

20 For illustrations of objects designed by Eugène

Feuillâtre, see *L'Art décoratif aux Expositions des Beaux-Arts*, Paris 1902, Plate 215; for André Fernand Thesmar, see *Ibid.*, Plate 221; for Raoul Wagner, see *L'Art décoratif aux Expositions des Beaux-Arts*, Paris 1903, Plate 179–80 and J. L. Bertrand, "Les Bijoux aux Salons de 1903," *Revue de la bijouterie, joaillerie, orfèvrerie*, Vol. 4, No. 40 (August 1903), 91–93.

21 C.R.C., "Accessions to the George E. Booth Collection," *Bulletin of the Detroit Institute of Arts*, Vol. 2, No. 1 (October 1920), 7–8. I would like to thank Nancy Rivard Shaw, curator of American Art at the Detroit Institute of Arts for sharing this information with me.

22 Tiffany & Co. silver pattern ledger, 1913–1914, n.p.

23 For illustration, see *Der Moderne Stil*, Vol. 4, No. 9 (1902), Plate 65, Fig. 7.

24 Quoted in Herwin Schaefer, *op cit.*, 312.

25 For listing of the painters who exhibited in Gallery 71, see *Official Catalogue of the Department of Fine Arts Panama-Pacific International Exposition*, San Francisco 1915, pp. 66–67.

26 "Exhibit of Louis Tiffany at the Panama-Pacific Exposition," *The Jewelers' Circular*, Vol. 70, No. 16 (19 May 1915), 41.

27 For illustration, see Paul E. Doros, *op. cit.*, p. 91, Plate 92.

28 "Exhibit of Louis Tiffany at the Panama-Pacific Exposition," *loc. cit.*

29 Quoted in Hugh F. McKean, *op. cit.*, p. 26.

30 I would like to thank C. Tiffany Bingham for sharing this information with me.

31 "Exhibit of Louis Tiffany at the Panama-Pacific Exposition," *loc. cit.*

32 Two catalogues for the Department of Fine Arts for the Panama-Pacific Exposition list only two copper vases, numbers 3460 and 3461. *Official Catalogue of the Department of Fine Arts Panama-Pacific International Exposition*, *op. cit.*, p. 67; and John E. D. Trask and J. Nilsen Laurvik, ed., *Catalogue De Luxe of the Department of Fine Arts Panama-Pacific International Exposition*, Vol. 2, San Francisco 1915, p. 375.

33 "Exhibit of Louis Tiffany at the Panama-Pacific Exposition," *loc. cit.*

34 *Ibidem.*

35 I would like to thank William Johnston at the Walters Art Gallery for sharing this information with me.

36 "Exhibit of Louis Tiffany at the Panama-Pacific Exposition," *loc. cit.*

37 Two Tiffany windows, "Parakeets and Goldfish Bowl" and "Feeding the Flamingoes," were exhibited at the 1893 World's Columbian Exposition in Chicago in a special room, known as the "Dark Room," which was decorated in shades ranging from pale yellow to dark bluish green, including the furnishings and embellishments in the room. "Tiffany Glass and Decorating Company's Exhibit at the Columbian Exposition," *The Decorator and Furnisher*, Vol. 23, No. 1 (October 1893), 10. For illustration of the "Parakeet and Goldfish Bowl" window, see *Synopsis of the Exhibit of the Tiffany Glass and Decorating Company in the American Section of the Manufactures and Liberal Arts Building at the World's Fair*, New York 1893, facing p. 4.

38 For illustration of the "Parakeets and Goldfish Bowl" window, see Alastair Duncan, Martin Eidelberg, and Neil Harris, *op. cit.*, Plate 62.

39 I would like to thank Thomas Paradise for his helpful insights into the intricacies in the enameling techniques employed in this tea screen.

40 See *Official Catalogue of the Department of Fine Arts Panama-Pacific International Exposition*, *op. cit.*, p. 67 and John E. D. Trask and J. Nilsen Laurvik, ed., *Catalogue De Luxe of the Department of Fine Arts Panama-Pacific International Exposition*, Vol. 2, p. 375.

41 "Exhibit of Louis Tiffany at the Panama-Pacific Exposition," *loc. cit.*

42 See *Official Catalogue of the Department of Fine Arts Panama-Pacific International Exposition*, *loc. cit.*, and *The Catalogue De Luxe of the Department of Fine Arts Panama-Pacific International Exposition*, *loc. cit.* Quoted in "Mr. Tiffany's Life Work in Art Here," *New York Herald*, 28 February 1916, microfilm, Archives of American Art Smithsonian, Louis Comfort Tiffany, Scrapbook, 01-249, p. 197.

43 "Exhibit of Louis Tiffany at the Panama-Pacific Exposition," *loc. cit.*

44 Quoted in Ben Macomber, *The Jewel City: Its Planning and Achievements; Its Architecture, Sculpture, Symbolism, and Music; Its Gardens, Palaces, and Exhibits*, San Francisco 1915, p. 118. I am grateful to Joseph Armstrong Baird who generously presented me with this book.

45 Tiffany had wanted to display his window, "The Bathers", at the Panama-Pacific Exposition, but the proper facilities for installing it at the Palace of Fine Arts were never made available. See "Tiffany Window to Stay Here," *American Art News*, 19 December 1914, microfilm, Archives of American Art Smithsonian-Louis Comfort Tiffany Scrapbook, 01-249, p. 56A.

46 The Tiffany & Co. Archives houses an "Agreement between Tiffany & Co. and Tiffany Studios," dated 26 March 1918, listing the following items which Tiffany & Co. agreed to provide to Tiffany Studios: 107 pieces of sterling silver holloware, 1160 pieces of sterling silver flatware (a service for 63) which were made from special dies, and 183 complementary serving pieces

made of silver-plated German silver. Nothing is known about this service or why it was ordered. Perhaps Tiffany was ordering items for his own personal use or for that of the Tiffany Studios.

47 Although this cup does not follow the exact lines of the chalice of Abbot Suger in the National Gallery of Art, Washington, D.C., it does bear an affinity with its use of gold and precious stones. For illustration, see Robert G. Calkins, *Monuments of Medieval Art*, New York 1979, p. 124, fig. 107.

48 This cup was offered in the Mrs. Henry Walters sale, *Art Collection of the Late Mrs. Henry Walters, op. cit.*, lot No. 736, p. 134 and listed as ''Eighteen-Karat Gold and Translucent Enamel Goblet.'' I would like to thank Vance Kohler for bringing this illustration to my attention.

49 *See 1909–1949 Records No. 2 T & Co.*, 18 June 1918, n.p. (Tiffany & Co. Archives).

50 For more information on the creation of the Tiffany Foundation, its objectives, the students who attended and its eventual demise, see Hugh F. McKean, *op. cit.*, pp. 265–69.

51 Quoted from brochure, Hobart Nichols, *Louis Comfort Tiffany Foundation*, Oyster Bay, Long Island, New York, no date, n.p.

52 The following jewelers studied at Laurelton Hall from 1920 to 1932: Paul Bogatay, Harold J. Brennan, Dorothy J. Diamond, Aime H. Doucette, Harold G. Griffith, Bruce Heiser, Estelle E. Kaiser, Edward R. Nelson, Edward E. Oakes, Dorothy Schmalhorst, Dorothy Schwab, Katherine Shuman, and Clayton T. Walker. Charles Price is the only silversmith listed. See *Art Guild Louis Comfort Tiffany Foundation*, 13th edition, Oyster Bay, Long Island, 1932, pp. 14–16. I would like to thank Lillian Nassau for sharing this privately printed booklet with me.

53 See Ezra Tharp, ''Iridescent Art,'' *The New Republic, A Journal of Opinion*, New York, Vol. 6, No. 74 (1 April 1916), 239.

54 See catalogue of retrospective exhibition, *The Art of Louis C. Tiffany*, New York 1916, Archives of American Art Smithsonian, Louis Comfort Tiffany, microfilm, Scrapbook, 01-249, p. 193.

55 See ''Mr. Tiffany's Life Work in Art Here,'' *New York Herald*, 28 February 1916, microfilm, Archives of American Art Smithsonian-Louis Comfort Tiffany Scrapbook, 01-249, p. 197.

Bibliography

Art Guild Louis Comfort Tiffany Foundation, 13th ed., Oyster Bay, New York, 1932. (Privately printed booklet)

The Arts of Louis Comfort Tiffany and His Times, exhibition catalogue, John and Mabel Ringling Museum of Art, Sarasota, Florida, 1975.

BECKER, Vivienne, *Art Nouveau Jewelry*, New York 1985.

BING, S., *Artistic America, Tiffany Glass and Art Nouveau*, reprint, introduction by Robert Koch, Cambridge, Massachusetts, 1970.

BURLINGHAM, Michael John, *The Last Tiffany: A Biography of Dorothy Tiffany Buringham*, New York 1989.

CARPENTER, Charles H., Jr. and Janet Zapata, *The Silver of Tiffany & Co. 1850–1987*, exhibition catalogue, Museum of Fine Arts, Boston 1987.

—— and Mary Grace, *Tiffany Silver*, New York, 1978.

CLARK, Robert Judson, ed., *The Arts and Crafts Movement in America 1876–1916*, Princeton, New Jersey, 1972.

COULDREY, Vivienne, *The Art of Louis Comfort Tiffany*, Secaucus, New Jersey, 1989.

CUMMING, Elizabeth and Wendy Kaplan, *The Arts and Crafts Movement*, New York/London 1991.

DEKAY, Charles, *The Art of Louis Comfort Tiffany*, New York 1914.

DOROS, Paul E., *The Tiffany Collection of the Chrysler Museum at Norfolk*, Norfolk, Virginia, 1978.

DUNCAN, Alastair, *Louis Comfort Tiffany*, New York 1992.

——, Martin Eidelberg and Neil Harris, *Masterworks of Louis Comfort Tiffany*, London/New York 1989.

——, *Tiffany at Auction*, New York 1981.

——, *Tiffany Windows*, London/New York 1980.

EIDELBERG, Martin, *E. Colonna*, exhibition catalogue, Dayton Art Institute, Musée des Arts Décoratifs de Montréal, The Renwick Gallery of the National Museum of American Art, Washington, D.C., 1983–84.

FELDSTEIN, William, Jr., and Alastair Duncan, *The Lamps of Tiffany Studios*, London/New York 1983.

FISHER, Alexander, *The Art of Enamelling upon Metal*, London 1906.

JANSON, Dora Jane, *From Slave to Siren: The Victorian Woman and Her Jewelry from Neoclassic to Art Nouveau*, exhibition catalogue, The Duke University Museum of Art, Durham, NC, 1971.

KOCH, Robert, *Louis Comfort Tiffany 1848–1933*, exhibition catalogue, The Museum of Contemporary Crafts of the American Craftsmen's Council, New York 1958.

——, *Louis C. Tiffany's Glass-Bronzes-Lamps A Complete Collector's Guide*, sixth printing, New York 1978.

——, *Louis C. Tiffany Rebel in Glass*, New York 1982.

LORING, John, *Tiffany's 150 Years*, New York 1987.

MARX, Roger, *La Décoration et les Industries d'Art à l'Exposition Universelle de 1900*, Paris 1900.

MCKEAN, Hugh F., *The "Lost" Treasures of Louis Comfort Tiffany*, New York 1980.

——, *The Treasures of Tiffany*, exhibition catalogue, Museum of Science and Industry, Chicago (from the collection of the Charles Hosmer Morse Foundation), 1982.

NEUSTADT, Dr. Egon, *The Lamps of Tiffany*, New York 1970.

The objects of Art of the Louis Comfort Tiffany Foundation, exhibition catalogue, Parke-Bernet Galleries, New York 1946.

POTTER, Norman and Douglas Jackson, *Tiffany Glassware*, New York 1988.

PRODDOW, Penny and Debra Healy, *American Jewelry, Glamour and Tradition*, New York 1987.

PURTELL, Joseph, *The Tiffany Touch*, New York 1971.

REYNOLDS, Gary, *Louis Comfort Tiffany: The Paintings*, exhibition catalogue, Grey Art Gallery and Study Center, New York University, 1979.

SAARINEN, Aline B. *The Proud Possessors*, New York 1958.

SATALOFF, Joseph, *Art Nouveau Jewelry*, Bryn Mawr, PA, 1984.

SCHNEIRLA, Peter and Penny Proddow, *Tiffany: 150 Years of Gems and Jewelry*, New York 1987.

SPEENBURGH, Gertrude, *The Arts of the Tiffanys*, Chicago 1956.

STOVER, Donald L., *The Art of Louis Comfort Tiffany*, exhibition catalogue, Fine Arts Museum of San Francisco (from the collection of the Charles Hosmer Morse Foundation), 1981.

TIFFANY & Co., *Blue Book*, advertising catalogues for years 1895–1920.

WEISBERG, Gabriel P. *Art Nouveau Bing Paris Style 1900*, New York, 1986.

WEITZENHOFFER, Frances, *The Havemeyers Impressionism Comes to America*, New York 1986.

Relevant articles

"American Art at the Turin Exposition," *The Jewelers' Circular and Horological Review*, Vol. 45, No. 8 (September 24, 1902), 1, 18; and (October 22, 1902), 48–49.

"The Art of the Modern Goldsmith," *Town and Country* (October 29, 1904), 16–17.

BELKNAP, Henry W., "Jewelry and Enamels," *The Craftsman*, Vol. IV, No. 3 (June 1903), 178–80.

BROWNELL, William C., "Decoration of the Seventh Regiment Armory," *Scribner's Monthly*, Vol. 22, No. 3 (July 1881), 371–80.

BURKE, Doreen Bolger, "Louis Comfort Tiffany and His Early Training at Eagleswood, 1862–1865," *The American Art Journal*, Vol. 19, No. 3 (1987).

DE QUELIN, René, "A Many-Sided Creator of the Beautiful," *Arts and Decoration*, Vol. 17, No. 3 (July 1922), 176–77.

EIDELBERG, Martin, "Tiffany's Early Glass Vessels," *The Magazine Antiques*, Vol. 137, No. 2, 502–15.

"Exhibit of Louis Tiffany at the Panama-Pacific Exhibition," *The Jewelers' Circular*, Vol. 70, No. 16 (May 19, 1915), 41.

"Exhibition Notes," *The China Decorator*, Vol. 25, No. 4 (April 1900), 92.

FAUDE, Wilson H., "Associated Artists and the American Renaissance in the Decorative Arts," *Winterthur Portfolio 10* (1975), 101–30.

FELD, Stuart, "Nature in Her Most Seductive Aspect: Louis Comfort Tiffany's Favrile Glass," *Bulletin of the Metropolitan Museum of Art*, Vol. 21 (November 1962), 100–12.

GENSEL, Walther, "Tiffany Gläser auf der Pariser Welt-Ausstellung 1900," *Deutsche Kunst und Dekoration*, Vol. VI (November 1900), 86–96.

HARLOW, Katherina, "A Pioneer Master of Art Nouveau: The Hand-wrought Jewellery of Louis C. Tiffany," *Apollo*, Vol. 116, No. 245 (July 1982), 46–50.

HOWE, Samuel, "Enamel As a Decorative Agent,"

The Craftsman, Vol. 2, No. 2 (May 1902), 61–68.

"The Jeweler's Craft: New Ideas in the Art which Makes Use of Precious Gems and Metals," *Washington Life*, Vol. III, No. 19 (November 5, 1904) 17–18.

KING, Polly, "Women Workers in Glass at the Tiffany Studios," *Art Interchange*, Vol. 33, No. 4 (October 1894), 86–88.

LANCASTER, Clay, "Oriental Contributions to Art Nouveau," *The Art Bulletin*, Vol. 34 (1952), 297–310.

"Louis C., Tiffany and His Work in Artistic Jewellery," *The International Studio*, Vol. 30, No. 117 (November 1906), xxxii–xlii.

"Notable Exhibits at the St. Louis Exposition. Part 1, Jewelry, by L. C. Tiffany," *The Jewelers' Circular Weekly*, Vol. 49, No. 13 (October 26, 1904), 16, 18, 20.

NOVAS, Himilce, "A Jewel in His Crown," *Connoisseur* (October 1983) 134–36, 138, 140.

SCHAEFER, Herwin, "Tiffany's Fame in Europe," *The Art Bulletin*, Vol. 44, No. 4 (December 1962), 309–28.

TEALL, Gardner C., "The Art of Things," *Brush and Pencil*, Vol. 4 (September 1899), 302–11.

——, "Artistic American Wares at Exposition," *Brush and Pencil*, Vol. 6. No. 4 (July 1900), 176–80.

THARP, Ezra, "Iridescent Art," *The New Republic A Journal of Opinion*, Vol. VI, No. 74 (April 1, 1916), 239–40.

TIFFANY, Louis C., "Color and Its Kinship to Sound," *The Art World*, Vol. II, No. 2 (May 1917), 142–44.

"Tiffany and Company at the St. Louis Exposition, *The Craftsman*, Vol. VII, No. 2 (November 1904), 169–83.

"The Tiffany Display at Paris," *The Art Interchange*, Vol. 44, No. 5 (May 1900), 112–13.

"Tiffany Glass and Decorating Company's Exhibit at the Columbian Exposition," *The Decorator and Furnisher*, Vol. 23, No. 1 (October 1893), 9–11.

"The Tiffany Glass at the Pan American," *Keramic Studio*, Vol. III, No. 2 (June 1901), 30–31.

"Tiffany's St. Louis Exhibit," *The Boston Budget*, Vol. XXXIV, No. 47 (November 19, 1904), 11.

TOWNSEND, Horace, "American and French Applied Art at the Grafton Galleries," *The International Studio*, Vol. 8, July 1899, 39–44.

"Die Turiner Ausstellung: Die Sektion Amerika," *Dekorative Kunst*, Vol. XI (October 1902), 49–55.

WAERN, Cecilia, "The Industrial Arts of America: the Tiffany Glass and Decorative Co.," *The Studio: An Illustrated Magazine of the Fine and Applied Art*, Vol. XI, No. 2 (September 1897), 156–65.

——, "The Industrial Arts of America: II, The Tiffany or 'Favrile' Glass," *The Studio*, Vol. XIV, No. 63 (June 1898), 16–21.

WEIR, Hugh, "Through the Rooking Glass – An Interview with Louis C. Tiffany," *Collier's*, Vol. 75, No. 21 (May 23, 1925) 10–11, 50–51.

"Wonderful Altar of Mosaic and Precious Stones in the Crypt of the Cathedral of St. John the Divine, New York," *The Jewelers' Circular*, Vol. 72, No. 4 (February 23, 1916), 39, 41.

ZAPATA, Janet, "Authenticating Tiffany Jewelry," *Jewelers' Circular Keystone* (August 1988), 226–30.

Photographic credits

(Color photos by number, black-and-white by page number.)

Allentown Art Museum: 79, 80, p. 138

Dirk Bakker: p. 176

David Behl: 65, 71

The Brooklyn Museum: 3

Christie's, New York: 1, 8, 10, 14, 38, 48, 58, 73, p. 38, p. 130

The Chrysler Museum: 26, p. 58, p. 66

The Corning Museum of Glass: p. 70

Nicholas Dawes: 7

William Doyle Galleries: 58, p. 107

Alastair Duncan: 13, 22, p. 160

Theodore Flagg: 9, 16, 47, 55, 56, 59, 61, 63, 72, 78, 83, p. 24, p. 34, p. 36, p. 39, p. 58, p. 62, p. 65, p. 72, p. 93, p. 134

Richard Goodbody: 11, 19, 27, 28, 32, 34, 35, 44, 45, 53, 54, 57, 66, 67, 69, 70, 80, p. 46, p. 47, p. 59, p. 60, p. 61, p. 64, p. 65, p. 69, p. 71, p. 92, p. 103, p. 104, p. 106, p. 109, p. 131, p. 134, p. 138

Library of Congress, Veterans of 7th Regiment Armory, New York: p. 28

Los Angeles County Museum of Art: 15

Metropolitan Museum of Art: 18, 20, 21, 24, 36, 49, p. 30, p. 31, p. 32, p. 33

Museum of Fine Art, Boston: 84

The Museum of Modern Art, New York: 12

New York Public Library: p. 34, p. 77, p. 79, p. 90

David Robinson: 37, 46, 50, 51, 64, 74, 76, p. 110, p. 155

Robert Skinner Gallery: 5

Sotheby's Inc.: 2, 17

Town and Country: p. 78

Townsend Photo: 25, 43

Michael Tropea: 60, 68, p. 110

University of Michigan Museum of Art: 6, 41, p. 34

Virginia Museum of Fine Arts: 23, 29, 31, 32

Walters Art Gallery: 42, 81

Acknowledgments

Writing a book is somewhat like putting together a jigsaw puzzle where scattered pieces must be arranged into a cohesive whole. Bits of information or odd objects which at first did not seem to fit into the general scheme of Louis Comfort Tiffany's work in jewelry and enamels suddenly made sense after a conversation with a collector, museum curator, or auction house expert. To these individuals, who provided many of the missing parts to my puzzle, I am immensely grateful.

Martin Eidelberg, my former professor at Rutgers University and friend, has been a constant support since the first time we discussed my preliminary findings several years ago, providing not only moral support but also introducing me to collectors who had a treasure trove of objects. I am also grateful to Tiffany & Co. who, over the years, have preserved valuable archival material. During my tenure as archivist, the company made this material available to all serious researchers in the field. Alastair Duncan and his assistant, Mary Beth McCaffrey, have been a source of knowledge, patiently answering my many questions and suggesting many collectors who could be helpful.

Dr. Hugh McKean has enriched the decorative arts field by assembling an extensive collection of Louis Comfort Tiffany's works at the Charles Hosmer Morse Museum of American Art. Through his generosity I had access to this collection as a well-spring from which I could draw again and again. David Donaldson, curator at the Museum, provided insights into the technical aspects of many of Tiffany's works, especially the fine art of enameling on metals. Jonathan Snellenburg of Christie's and Katie Leong and Jean Lichtenstein, two practising jewelers, helped unravel the key to the complexities of the various enameling techniques on the objects that Tiffany placed on loan to the Metropolitan Museum of Art. Thomas Paradise, an author and lecturer on the subject, explained the enameling intricacies on the tea screen which Tiffany exhibited in the 1915 Panama-Pacific Exposition. Ubaldo Vitali described the process involved in forming copper vessels.

Shelton Barr and Thomas Gardner at Barr-Gardner in New York City generously made available to me their extensive collection of auction catalogues as well as their research material on the subject. Simon Teakle, Nancy McClelland and Usha Subramaniam of Christie's; Berj Zavian and Susan Abeles of William Doyle Galleries; Gloria Lieberman and Louise Luther of Skinner's; and Barbara Deisroth, Kevin Tierney and Ian Irving of Sotheby's, not only shared information but also provided me with access to their library of illustrative material.

Many museum curators allowed me access to their collections, opening their files and answering my numerous questions: Peter Blume, Allentown Art Museum; Mark Clark and Gary Baker, Chrysler Museum, Norfolk, Virginia; Nancy Rivard Shaw, The Detroit Institute of Arts; Leslie Greene Bowman, Los Angeles County Museum of Art; Alice Cooney Frelinghuysen, Metropolitan Museum of Art; Christopher Mount, The Museum of Modern Art, New York City; Lisa Weilbacker, the Seventh Regiment Armory, New York City; Frederick Brandt, Virginia Museum of Fine Arts, Richmond, Virginia; and William Johnston, Walters Art Gallery, Baltimore, Maryland; Kevin Stayton, The Brooklyn Museum; Norma Jenkins, Corning Museum of Glass; and Terry Kerby, University of Michigan Museum of Art, provided valuable illustrative material.

Many friends and colleagues contributed in innumerable ways to this book: Dr. Joseph Armstrong Baird; Brian Albert and Joseph Ahumada; Rosalie Berberian, Ark Antiques; C. Tiffany Bingham; Nicholas M. Dawes; Janet and Byrd Drucker; Ralph Esmerian; Martha Gandy Fales; Audrey Friedman, Primavera Gallery; Ray and Lee Grover; Jonathan Hallam; Natalie Z. Helander; Kathryn Hobart, Hobart-Lyon Appraisals; Wallace Janowski, Wallace Refiners; Gwendolyn Kelso; Vance Koehler; Sylvia Kornblum, Team Antiques; Lynne and Michael Lerner; Jacques Limacher; Barbara Macklowe, Lawrence Matlick and Frank Maraschiello, Macklowe Gallery & Modernism; Geoffrey C. Munn, Wartski; Paul Nassau, Harry Wallace and Arlie Sulka, Lillian Nassau Ltd.; Andrew Nelson and Malcolm Logan, Nelson Rarities; Penny Proddow; Crary Pullen, Town & Country; Oscar Riedener; Len Rothe; Dr. Joseph and Ruth Sataloff; Benedict Silverman; Sandra and Nat Silverman; D. Albert Soeffing; Werner Sonn, The Henri Stern Watch Agency; Gerald Unger; and Michael Weller, Argentum.

I owe special thanks to Lillian Nassau, whose expertise in the Art Nouveau field is legendary; Ira Simon, whose enthusiasm for my book almost matched my own; Neil Lane, who always found yet another wonderful piece; Gladys and Robert Koch, who kindly shared their knowledge of Tiffany; Judy Cohen of J. M. Cohen Rare Books, who always seemed to anticipate my next request; George Harlow at the American Museum of Natural History, who patiently answered my many gemological questions; Paula and Howard Ellman, who graciously allowed me access to their wonderful collection; Carol Ferrante, who immediately became excited about my project after our first meeting; Micki and Jay Doros, who shared their love of Tiffany; Ruth Caccavale, my former assistant at Tiffany's, who located several pertinent drawings in the Archives; and Henry Platt, former President and Chairman of Tiffany & Co., who was a delight to converse with about his illustrious great-great-grandfather, Louis Comfort Tiffany.

I am especially indebted to my editor, Stanley Baron of Thames and Hudson, who gently prodded me when I reached an impasse and understood my turmoil when my mother became ill and died during the writing of this book.

But the person to whom I am most grateful is my husband, Ricardo, who kept his belief in me. His untiring editorial advice provided an objective perspective whenever I could no longer see the forest for the trees.

Index   *(Italic numbers refer to color illustrations.)*

DATE DUE